MINDING
THE DARKNESS

129
140

Some Other Books by
PETER DALE SCOTT

POETRY*

Coming to Jakarta: A Poem About Terror
Listening to the Candle: A Poem on Impulse
Crossing Borders: Selected Shorter Poems

TRANSLATION

Zbigniew Herbert: Selected Poems
(with Czeslaw Milosz)

PROSE

The War Conspiracy
Crime and Cover-Up
Cocaine Politics
The Iran-Contra Connection
Deep Politics and the Death of JFK

* Available from New Directions

PETER DALE SCOTT

MINDING
THE DARKNESS

A POEM FOR THE YEAR 2000

Book Three of
Seculum: A Trilogy

A NEW DIRECTIONS BOOK

Manufactured in the United States of America
New Directions Books are printed on acid-free paper
First published as New Directions Paperbook 906 in 2000
Published simultaneously in Canada by Penguin Books Canada Limited

Author's Acknowledgments:
I want the world to know that this poem is, in its inception as in its end, a love poem to my wife Ronna Kabatznick.

I have not space to name all the friends to whom I am deeply indebted in the writing of this poem. But I wish to acknowledge the unique contribution of James Laughlin, who gave me not only the opportunity but above all the needed encouragement to complete this work of twenty years. American letters will not be the same without him.

I wish to thank Pramoedya Ananta Toer, his U.S. publisher Hyperion East, his translator Alex G. Bardsley, and *Indonesia*, for permission to quote extensively from Pramoedya Ananta Toer, trans. Alex G. Bardsley, *My Apologies, in the Name of Experience* [c. 1992], *Indonesia*, 61 (April 1996).

I wish to thank the Rockefeller Foundation, and especially the staff of the Bellagio Study and Conference Center, for the opportunity, in September-October 1997, to complete a working draft of *Minding the Darkness* at the Villa Serbelloni on Lake Como. This supplied an unexpected third lake to complement those in the two earlier volumes of my father (Lake Massawippi) and of my mother (deep in the Laurentians). My wife Ronna and I will always be grateful.

I would like also to acknowledge thankfully the journals in which portions of this volume were previously published: *Agni* (I.i-iii, II.i), *Canadian Literature* (II.ii, part of First Retreat), *Chicago Review* (III.v-vii), *Conjunctions* (IV.v, vii-ix), *Epoch* (IV.ii-iv), *FlashPoint* (II.iv-vi), *Harvard Review* (IV.x), *The Inquiring Mind* (part of First Retreat), *Malahat Review* (III.iv), *Manoa* (IV.xi), *McGill Law Journal* (part of First Retreat), *New American Writing* (III.ii,iv), *Notre Dame Review* (III.ix), *Partisan Review* (V.i), *Salmagundi* (II.iii), *Tikkun* (V.ii), *TriQuarterly* (II.x, Second Retreat), *Zyzzyva* (II.vii, II.xi, III.xii, IV.i, IV.vi).

Library of Congress Cataloging-in-Publication Data

Scott, Peter Dale.
    Minding the darkness: a poem for the year 2000 / Peter Dale Scott.
        p. cm. (New Directions paperbook ; 906)
    "Book three of seculum: a trilogy."
    Includes bibliographical references (p. 249)
    ISBN 0-8112-1454-0 (acid-free paper)
    1. Two thousand, A.D.—Poetry. 2. Millenium—Poetry. I. Title

PR9199.3.S364 M56 2000
811'.54—dc21

                        00-055415

New Directions Books are published for James Laughlin
by New Directions Publishing Corporation
80 Eighth Avenue, New York 10011

Dedicated with love
to my wife Ronna

CONTENTS

HUN LUAN—DARK CONFUSION

"When Tao does not prevail in the world, war horses thrive in
the suburbs"
                                                    —Tao Te Ching 46

"The Last Law is the time of the destruction of the teaching"
                                                    —Lotus Sutra, Chapter XIV

"When you see the blackness like this, then you will know
this blackness is the beginning of your work."
                                                    —Mirror of the Philosophers

"Wo aber Gefahr ist, wächst/ Das Rettende auch" ("Yet where
danger is,/ Grows also what saves")
                                    —Hölderlin '52 216–17; Heidegger '49 255–56

I.i

If you want to change your life
      burn down your house
   Before we left for the beach   *10/20/91*

Ronna took off her rings
            placing them on the basin
   to be safe like her other possessions

the hot offshore winds
            meant it was warm and cool
   as we waded on the wet sand

through the agitated air
            a day that was just right
   Ronna rehearsing her solemn

procession toward me
            one arm crooked up
   on her imaginary father's

the other with an imaginary bouquet
            surrounded by frisbees
   a day happy enough

to forgive one's karma
            forget that of others
   under a blue sky

which as we returned
            over the Devil's Slide
   was divided like a flag

half blue half ominous black
            the dense smoke a message
      to speed home

over the Bay Bridge
            to the miles-wide storm cloud
      increasing in darkness

fringed with dots of flame
            until it was almost night
      headlights the sudden emergency

warning our freeway was *CLOSED*
            towards the house where
      (we did not yet know this)

Cherry our unsuspecting
            house-mate from Taiwan
      had just narrowly escaped

through a burning rain
            of eucalyptus leaves
      with no more than her stuffed bear

and a few yards up the street
            eight people burned to death
      rivulets of metal

from their melted cars
            over the burned asphalt
      We were the last to make it through

we heard from one survivor
            who had jumped in the back
      of a stranger's pick-up

in the hushed exchanges
            as we waited for coffee
      next morning at the bed-and-breakfast

with nothing to do that day
            but to tell our tales
            (the woman two doors down

had loaded her car to the roof
            and now it was too late
            to go back inside

and find her car keys)
            tales that were fragments
            The fourth afternoon

we were taken there
            in an Oakland police car
            a wreath where our neighbor died

and the thick layer of ash
            (Could this be all our books?
            the stove?   the refrigerator?

the two sets of china?)
            as unpossessed
            as the Huron potsherds

in the black corner of an autumn˙field
            the burnt tiles of that Roman villa—
            impossible to explain this

for a world not fully mindful
            that we all must die
            In a bravura gesture

of letting-go
            Ronna took out her key
            and threw it back to the Devas

we were taken away
            the three of us crying
            like ancient warriors

5

or pre-adolescents
              dry sobs that since
         have come back in therapy

divorce my mother's death
              choked us that week
         at each glimpse of the naked hillside

as labile as children
              who have not yet the illusion
         we are in control

dazzled and shattered in turn
              by the ominous beauty
         of say a sunset under rainclouds

from which it was a relief
              to go back to teaching
         Pound's tears at Pisa

watching the spider at work
              the tent-peg's moving shadow
         the moon through laundry

to the nine-through-fiveness
              of a twentieth century
         the unquestioned defense of a self

as if in one week
              we had lived two different ages
         two habits of living

the comfort of Culture
              more easily destroyed than preserved
         versus *Dasein face to face*

with its original nakedness   *Heidegger '90 291; Safranski 187*
              the two irreconcilable
         except when caught off guard

my cheek unexpectedly wet
>from reading in the *Chronicle*
of Tibetan prayer flags

flapping
from the remains of trees   San Francisco Chronicle 11/29/91

I.ii

They do not know me
but swarm to the bread
I toss out by the creekside

the brash ones supping at my feet
even the shy one
my heart goes out to

cocking his head at me
>from behind the elm-trunk
Why is it so much harder

to gain the understanding
of friends? I wonder
having once again escaped

to eat here alone
>from the crowded tables
of Faculty Club colleagues

one of them (far more intelligent
than most in his field)
having just really hurt me

in the midst of my unaccustomed
vulnerability
by calling my big speech

over twenty years ago
           in the Greek Theater
       for closing the university

in response to the Cambodian invasion
           (my swan song as it were
       to the collapsing Movement)

your eulogy of Pol Pot!
           What hope for human discourse?
       I can feel no loss

that my best political files
           have all burned
       if their message is too complex

even for close Harvard-educated
           friends with Ph.D.'s
       But in a world so ill-governed

one cannot as Socrates said
           think much of its teachers
       just as the birds' presence

here in front of my shoes
           does not make them disciples
       their calculated trust

not so commendable
           as I once believed
       For six months the Cousteaus

fed a sea-otter at Monterey
           and then when they had left
       it came up to someone else

who shot it
           We who live in cities
       like to talk of *nature*

and *ecological balance*
    of deeper patterns
   than what we see

miraculous stories
    usually from far off
   of a ferry going down in flames

a dolphin rescuing a survivor
    We want to believe them
   when we see the TV news

Serbs shelling Dubrovnik
    dozens of buildings destroyed   *11/4/91*
   scenes which one week ago

revived the survivors' guilt
    I have carried since World War II
   that humanity is the problem

that this century's disasters
    anticipated by Nietzsche
   a convulsion of earthquakes

wars the like of which
    have never been seen on earth   *Nietzsche '69 #1; Sluga 49*
   followed not from *weakness of the will*   *Nietzsche '87 #43; Sluga 47*

but from its opposite   willful
    disruption for sake of profit
   of small-scale ecosystems

we thought four years of drought
    last year's heavy frost
   the dead hillside eucalyptus

were all somehow *unnatural*
    that with a native cover
   of redwood and live oak

we might have been spared the fire
        the ash which has killed the fish
    in Lake Temescal

from my books   my car
        from *thirty-three hundred homes*
    many more than Dubrovnik

barely a *soupçon*
        of what happens in modern wars
    and yet enough to give us

what most Americans have forgotten
        a taste of what it was like
    to endure the burning

of Washington or Atlanta   *1814 C.E., 1864 C.E.*
        or   as ten years later
    my mind restored by distance

to its usual thinking
        secure in denial
    can read of the first millennium's

earthquakes followed by fires
        when London and Oxford burned   *982 C.E., 1010 C.E.*
    Hamburg and Córdoba   *844 C.E., 1010 C.E.*

in one hour   laid waste   *Rev 18:17*
        inspiring a monk
    (*Alas   the great city!*)   *Rev 18:9*

to warn of *perilous times*
        covetousness stalks abroad
    the whole human race

sliding into the gulf   *Rodulfus Glaber: Patrologia Latina 142.635*
        of primeval chaos   *Reston 94, 155, 205*
    having seen annihilation

can one believe again
　　　　in Wordsworthian *ministries?*
　　　odd how much time there is

now my car has melted
　　　　I have less control of my life
　　　and my life less over me

I don't keep up
　　　　as much as I used to
　　　even these chickadees

are too nervous for me
　　　　there is no answer here
　　　a quick flutter in the stream

and they are gone

I.iii

I believe in enmindment
　　　　the translation of light
　　　into awareness of the dark

and understanding of that fear
　　　　we return to
　　　whenever we forget

Last autumn the brilliant
　　　　sunsets of deep merlot red
　　　from Mount Pinatubo in the Philippines

sensuous in the distance
　　　　if also ominous
　　　a reminder of how much

11

urbanization deludes us
>to think *we control our lives*
>peasants under a volcano

know perhaps better what they are doing
>as they plant their rice in furrows
>than Ronna and I who lived

among a lifetime of belongings
>we thought (wrongly)
>we could count our own

and then through the weeks
>I sifted the meager ashes
>vainly for her diamond ring

that lifetime complacency
>suddenly converted to
>the opposite much older nostalgia

we can control nothing
>a reminiscence of childhood's
>uncontrollable disasters

and finally a humbled insight
>about moments in time
>not being strung together

for you to rely on
>as did the Enlightenment
>inspired by science to engineer

new projects for humane
>and rational community
>whose failure now in Eastern Europe

has been followed so soon
>by the resurgence
>of old hatreds too long denied

churches destroying churches
          with that rage aroused uniquely
     by visions of peace

divine Leninist or pragmatic
          from the seminary the Sorbonne
     or the National War College

but humbled and liberated
          by the fluke of fire
     one has the perspective to see

that the Enlightenment
          was so much more constricted
     and unenlightened than we had thought

needing to define
          and then eradicate
     any available demon

church state or class
          to explain why the world was not
     what we intended it to be

the brightness of Voltaire
          who mocked Dante
     for having made Virgil say

his parents were Lombards   *Inferno 1.68*
          (exactly the same as
     if Homer were to announce

he had been born a Turk)   *Farinelli 2.217*
          the Voltaire who was sure
     he knew better than they did

what was good for the Jews
          and who died cursing
     écrasez l'infame

behind the Soviet philanthropy
        which sought to eradicate faith
    by use of an Inquisition

and also that of the West
        and its priesthoods of social science
    who after decades of pressing

unwanted dams and military
        torturers on the Third World
    have helped *liberate* the Soviet Union

for a new world order
        of Schumpeterian destructiveness
    whose outcome is *not yet*

the zeals of the early
        and the late Christianity
    the early they died for

the late they killed for
        still driving Enlightenment's
    late crusades against infidels

in the name of revolution
        or (in our local dialect)
    economic development

Thus now to overlook
        the zeals of Enlightenment
    would contribute to its decay

just as to fault enlightenment
        for its lack of kinship with the dark
    is to think critically once again

I believe in enmindment
        and poetic politics
    the intuition of an agenda

not just from the past
        still less from some nihilistic
   assertion of pure possibility

but from the familiar silence
        of a source beyond *self*
   accessible to anyone

liberated from possession
        like Ronna and myself
   now my best files from two decades

are ashes on a hillside
        I can look to Dante
   who precisely because

he was a *parte per se stesso*   *party unto himself; Paradiso 17.68-69*
        exile and fugitive
   seeking a path between

the *ordinata caritas* of faith   *ordered love*
        and the Kantian *sapere aude*   *dare to know;*
   (the heroic pursuit of knowledge   *Kant 54; Horace Epod. 1,2,40*

that led Odysseus to drowning)   *Inferno 26.120, 142*
can speak to us

II

YANG

"When a country is ill-governed, riches and honour are things to be ashamed of"
—Confucius, *Analects* 8.13.3

"The historian relates the events which have happened, the poet those which might happen."
—Aristotle, *Poetics* 9.2

Ben puoi veder che la mala condotta
  è la cagion che'l mondo ha fatto reo
  e non natura che'n voi sia corrotta.

"Thou canst see plainly that ill-guiding is the cause that has made the world wicked, and not nature that is corrupt in you."
—Dante, *Purgatorio* 16.103–05

"Uns selber zu verstehn! Das ists, was uns emporbringt."
("To understand ourselves! That is what raises us up.")
—Hölderlin '22 194; Hölderlin '52 23

II.i

To deal with the living
> we must talk more bravely with the dead
> not just any dead but the dearest

those who learned long ago
> like Dante and Tu Fu
> from the complicities of war and madness

to converse less with neighbors
> than with the dead before them
> making it easier

to accept the living for what they mostly are
> and are not   kind apparitions
> in a crowded hallway with whom

it is better to exchange just kindly words
> saving true anger and despair
> for God and the other major authors

of massacre   When Sharon and I went walking   *Sharon Dahl*
> up the fragrant path above the highway
> through orange groves at first but then

out into the cooler chaparral
> I kept pushing ahead as usual but she stopped
> we both stopped   and we heard above

the faint featureless rush
> from the glinting automobiles
> the far-off dog in the valley

the crickets
        the occasional portentous bumblebees
    for her (I think) all former humans

in some stricken or perhaps happier karma
        for me the instantaneous
    conspiracy of everything alive

sharing in joy that moment already gone
        that surface of all that had gone before
    the pendant wild currant blossoms

fallen   This morning having read
        a living poet I had never heard of
    the Syrian Muhammed al-Maghut

when only asphalt separates the corpses
        from the shoes of pedestrians   al-Maghut 232
    I am given the voice to tell my parents

(for this is a poem to my parents)
        I love you and you are dead   F.R. Scott d. 1/31/85
    and closer to me than before   M.D. Scott d. 11/28/93

and whether you are or maybe not
        united with the souls from El Mozote   site of El Salvador army
    you confirm me in my perverse obsession   massacre 12/81

with the world's perversities of power
        against those who gathered as instructed
    to the refuge of their church

in those hills you see from the AeroNica plane
        to be slaughtered by the taxes of the kindly   New Yorker
    those too gentle to worry overmuch   12/6/93

what is this darkness that governs us
        Often if I awaken in the night
    it is because I hear voices

20

of other dead   I dreamt two nights ago
          that at a meeting of the English Department
     the old were talking of their predecessors

who had made them who they were   and in the dream
          I sobbed   as recently once or twice
     I sobbed for you as I had never before

(at least while sane) knowing in the dream
          I sobbed not because we must die
     but partly out of generous respect

for this veneration   partly because
          those few students who might in good time come
     to venerate me will never I know teach here

they have done what I told them and are jobless
          (just as my son Mika put a good life first
     just as I told him and for years was almost jobless)

what use here could be the skill I taught
          (perhaps I should say the skill that I was taught)
     of having converse with those other failures

Ovid cursing from the Crimea
          Dante on the feverish Adriatic
     Pound soiling himself with his pollutions

in fury as the machinations of old men
          prepared for still more hunger and more war?
     On that path we were little more than strangers

yet peace came so easily to us   Must one
          truly be distraught as those men were
     to converse with the crickets

voices in the blue air?

II.ii

For Frank Scott (August 1, 1899–January 31, 1985)

As an only child
              whose father was often absent
       I studied his ways

not just on fishing trips
              when from the back of the canoe
       he showed how to twist the paddle

silently in the water
              so as not to scare the loon
       or when at Lachute

how to make the boomerang
              float back through the air
       to drop at our feet

I remember his netted sling
              I thought of him as David
       when the round pebble sailed

far over the cedars
              At that time I knew little
       of my father's ideals

drawn from moral critiques
              of *the acquisitive society*   *Djwa 51, 138*
       or after he came to believe

the orthodox was wrong   *Djwa 82*
              his more practical proposals
       for *politics*

the only road to heaven now   *Djwa 117*
              having learnt from H.G. Wells
       that misery could be replaced

by imagination and large-scale planning   Djwa 96
        But in his absences
    at meetings to make things better

using law as an instrument
        to reshape Canada
    through the CCF Party   *Cooperative Commonwealth Federation*

I knew that he had angered
        with his dominant will
    not just the Montreal police

or the McGill Board of Governors
        when he spoke up against
    the attack with truncheons

on the march of the unemployed
        but sometimes friends and allies
    Why even he confessed

how when he and his brothers
        camped in the wild country
    up the Murray River

they would climb to a cliff top
        and topple huge boulders
    to crash through the forest beneath

(a side to the law professor
        and defender of human rights
    against the excesses

of the Prime Minister of Quebec
        not everyone knew about
    he candidly admitted

that even in wilderness
        you couldn't be certain
    there was no one else around)

It must have been Frank who showed
        how to rock a rotting tree trunk
    slowly backwards and forwards

finding and feeding the rhythm
        that would finally bring it down
    in a chaos of broken branches

and the first time I did it on my own
        in front of three young girls
    as the pine began to fall

there leapt out from a hole near the top
        one two three four five   a whole family
    of flying squirrels

as I looked in the feral eyes
        of the middle sister
    I saw myself as demiurge

and believed for a moment with Goethe
        that to discover the mysteries
    of nature one must violate them

Was there something in our line
        that was tempted by decay
    to bring it crashing down?

When after Kent State
        and Nixon's invasion of Cambodia
    I moved the faculty amendment

to suspend all campus teaching
        and the Governor responded in rage
    did I pause even for a second

to ask What have we wrought?
        and though by acting out
    that particular drama I still believe

we avoided the violence
        that divided teachers from students
    at Harvard and Columbia

I have finally seen this moment
        why Milosz remembering
    the gangs of Central Europe

turned his back on me then
        the same year my father
    in the *crise d'octobre*   *Quebec crisis 1970*

counseled Pierre Trudeau
        to invoke the War Measures Act
    and for the sake of law

to suspend due process
        while rounding up leaders and poets
    even the singer Pauline Julien

who lived near us in North Hatley
        and sang at that anti-war rally
    My mother who like myself

took the part of those arrested
        understood better than my father
    that his paranoid fear

(giving her a U.S. fifty dollar bill
        and saying *Meet me in Rouse's Point*
    across the border

if we get separated
        and if the rioters
    have not closed all the bridges

off Montreal island)
        went back to that week of terror
    Quebec City in 1917

six days of martial law
>from the conscription riots
>and before that the gangs speaking *joual*   *québecois*

that used to wait for him
>on his way home from school
>his memories of violence

creating respect for law
>just as too much respect for law
>from citizens who behave

like folks in a Milgram experiment
>can unleash new violence
>till states become engines

of self-fulfilling paranoia
>driving peoples apart
>I remember my father's sling

it was just before she died
>my mother told me
>how police had come to the door

of St. Matthew's Rectory
>in the Upper Town of Quebec
>to show my grandfather the Archdeacon

the stone that had broken a window
>in the French-speaking Lower Town
>the same year my father   *1917*

obsessed with the explosiveness
>of guns and gunpowder
>stuffed one with the other

yanked the trigger with a long string
>to which nothing happened
>till all at once the gun

blew up in his arms and face
        not even the special train
    from his uncle the Vice-President

of the Grand Trunk Railway
        that took him from Quebec to Montreal
    could save his eye and his ear

Nothing not even the fire
        has affected me like that
    I escaped in World War Two

when by accident I bicycled
        through the middle of what turned out later
    to have been a conscription riot

with no worse than catcalls after me
        and I have learned from experience
    to see how a rotting pine trunk

may be someone's home
        how it may be fate
    and not merely character

that makes an Apollonian
        defense of the law
    turn to extra-legal power

while my father a rugged
        and sensitive man
    beloved by many

though usually from outside
        with a mind sometimes benign
    or else volcanic with frustration

from his failure to build
        the Blakean commonwealth
    of the Anglican Hymnal

I will not cease from mental strife
        Till we have built Jerusalem
    a poet with his own voice

and in the end that older voice
        speaking in Wordsworth's dream   *Prelude* 5.93-99
    of apocalyptic deluge   F.R.Scott 51

approached his death struggling
        with almost prophetic forces
    inside of him

never to be fulfilled

II.iii

What does it mean
        that one of Dante's sinners
    and an arhat in a tanka from Tibet   *arhat: Holy one* (Mahayana Buddhism)
                                         tanka: religious painting

each stalks towards us
        holding his severed head
    by a twist of its shocked hair?

I once was trained to aver
        against instinct these were proofs
    of trade along the Silk Route

which I had hoped to trace again
        from Dunhuang to Samarkand
    in that brief interval

after the Vietnam War
        before the resumption of the tribal feuds
    (not all cultures are textual

but have we not now nostalgia
          for tribes and their small
     ecologies of violence?)

with Franz who had lived two years   *Franz Schurmann*
          among the shepherds he studied
     under the snowcrests of the Pamirs

and now wrote columns
          of global analysis
     published in Arabic and Japanese

Much later I surmised
          it was the art of Gandhara
     the first human portraits

from the cult of godly Alexander
          transferred to the cult of Buddha
     (and King Milander the Bodhisattva)

in the halos we now expect
          from Lhasa to Vezelay
     that descended in due time

from the saviors to the martyrs
          and other witnesses
     to the fallibility of the world

just as the hot dismemberments
          in the black purgatories
     of Ireland and Korea

used kitchen spit and skillet
          for those horrors which have obsessed
     all visioning saintliness

even pilgrims to east and west
          Fa Xian and Prester John
     weavers of text-history

albeit it was only
        trade routes they traveled by
    But what does it mean

that in the thirteenth century
        three Tendai monks in Japan
    Shinran Dogen and Nichiren   *d. 1262, 1253, 1282 C.E.*

all believed *the decline of the dharma*   *mo fa*
        (which Gil the Norwegian-
    American Zen priest who married us

says arose from no more
        than a scribal error in Chinese)   *Nattier 90-118*
    had already arrived

all three threw over the codes
        of measure and prohibition
    that had structured the sangha   *Buddhist community*

for something radically simple:
        mantra   or *shikantaza (just sit)*   *Pure Land Buddhism;*
    or the practice of peace   *Soto Zen Buddhism; Nichiren Buddhism*

in the same era
        that in the Romagna
    the Abbot Joachim of Flora   *1132–1202 C.E.*

with learned calculation
        from biblical metaphor
    proclaimed that the age of the Son

which is to say the Church
        was like that of the Father and the Law
    in its final decline

bringing into play the radical
        forces of the Holy Spirit
    your sons and daughters shall prophesy

and your old men shall dream dreams?   Joel 2:28; Acts 2:17
    In the West first
  and then belatedly Japan

religious self-questioning
      produced Enlightenment
  first *the emergence*

from self-incurred immaturity
      (the inability to use
  one's understanding

without the guidance of another)   Kant 54; Horkheimer and Adorno 85
    and then (*metamorphoses*
  of criticism

into affirmation)   Horkheimer and Adorno xii
    the Liberal revolution
  which *expelled the Jesuits*

converted churches to Masonic temples   Goldman 77
    allowing commerce not scripture
  to rule society

and hence the common world
    With Kant's affirmation
  of the scientific system

as the form of truth
    thought seals its own nullity   Horkheimer and Adorno 85
  One might imagine

that Hegel's grim blessing
    Was wirklich ist ist vernünftig   what is actual is rational;
  is an endorsement   Hegel '42 10

of our mindless banking system
    and endless defense budgets
  But *a crime* even for Hegel

is only *existence*
which is nullity at the core — *Hegel '75A 71; MacGregor '98 28*
How can we attune

our self-clouded intellects
to the mysteries of Tao
letting words themselves

and not those who transmit them
have their own cunning
their own unshakable dialectic

which must be tangled out
like recombinant DNA
or two sleeping lovers who in bed

once each has freely lapsed
to some abandoned posture
find the only places

where their hands can rest?
Let the words' cunning
die List der Vernunft — *the cunning of reason; Hegel '28 63*

(even the sutras say
Go beyond language) — *Bodhidharma 44*
be submitted to that of the smile

and empower one more time
the impulse *within us*
iconoclastic against

the pieties of the crowd
and of those poets who submit
to nothing more than language

die heimliche List
dieser verschwiegenen Erde
the secret cunning

II.iv

Unde hoc malum? Whence this evil?   *Brown 394*
            is a question for those
        in a point of vantage

outside the swirl of dialectics
            which has given us justice and the state
        and *great confusion*   *hun luan; Tao Te Ching 18*

in a time of expansion
            there is no such freedom
        in times of scaling down

the illusory separation
            of light and darkness
        is a theme for compassion

like the Poles in Warsaw
            each person carrying a candle
        in the broad river of candles

descending upon the graveyard
            of wax-smoke under the birches
        on the Night of the Dead

Our problematic answer
            is *Far! Very far!*
        the heavy cannon

on the hills above Sarajevo
            from centuries of reaction
        to the tyranny of the Turks

after Sultan Murad
        at the Battle of Kosovo
    liberated the Bogomils

from Christian persecution
        to enter the light of Islam
    as before them the Berber

Donatists *most of them country folk*
        who did not even know Latin   A.H.M Jones 2. 955
    rose up from the *latifundia*   *rural estates*

across North Africa
        to welcome the armies of the Vandals
    and after them Mohammed

It was Saint Augustine
        who made the painful decision
    to persecute them

and enforce the word with power
        (*Fearfulness and trembling are come over me*
    and horror overwhelmed me

and I said   *O that I had the wings of a dove*
        for then I would fly away   *Psalm 55:2*
    and be at rest   *Aug. Ep. 95, 3; Brown 243*

but nonetheless it was better
        that *a few perish in their own flames*
    than that all should burn in the flames of Hell!)   *Aug. Ep. 204. 2;*
                                                                    Brown 336

whose mother *Monnica* (*a Berber name*)   *Frend 230*
        had like the Donatist peasants
    set out food for the saints   *Augustine Confessions 6.2.1*

and even before that the decision
        to discover a fragment
    of the cross to conquer with

from the top to the bottom
            reverting a global message
      back to a tribal one

and where in such African regions
            as Hippo Diarrhytos (Bizerte)
      the Catholic landowners

would not trouble to hand Circumcellions
            over to Augustine to be 'instructed':
      they merely dealt with them on the spot   *Brown 241*

so there today the college-educated
            Algerian military junta
      still deal in like fashion with the Hamas

And where in the Middle East
            the persecutions of the Nestorians
      and Monophysites and Monotheletes

by the imperial Councils
            of Chalcedon and Constantinople   *451 C.E.; 680 C.E.*
      preceded the 19th-century

massacres of Maronites
            by the Hakimite Druses
      and most recently the displacement

of Lebanese moderates
            by the troops of the Phalange
      the murder of Bashir Gemayel

and retaliatory massacres
            in the Sabra and Shatila camps
      the bombing of the U.S. Marine barracks

Orthodoxy always the doctrine
            enforced with political power
      hence it always makes room

for the corrupting influence of state
    It is this legacy
that we in the East and West

have been left to believe in
        my father's belief in law
and hence in sovereignty

being what I lost that year
        with the post-war best and brightest
protecting the needs of our states

in the Third Committee
        against the spectre
of the U.N. Charter on Human Rights

no place to be mindful
        the other choice—Saint Martin
who chose to convert

from the bottom not the top
        the *pagani* of the countryside
whom Augustine never knew

Martin whose powers were weakened
        when he went in vain to the bishops
to plead for a heretic's life—   *Sulp. Sev. Dial. 2.13; Hoare 137*

by now the forgotten one
        In his place the Maoism
of the Long March

which answered millennia
        of mandarin indifference
to the fate of peasants

with the Cultural Revolution
        the armies of Tiananmen
and now the *Khmères Rouges*

killing people on highways
        for driving a motor car
    We have seen it

from Lebanon to Afghanistan
        where it decays to war
    of city against countryside

(the fatal weakness
        of Lenin's conspiratorial
    revolution at the top)

the countryside wins
        and what is proven
    is not the weakness of books

(the faith in leadership
        in the *Quotations* of the poet Mao
    is from the Book of Odes)

but of the cities' loss
        of restraint by words
    till the rich compete

to impoverish the poor
        Those who search for *evil*   *Brown 394*
    (which is the excuse for power)

reducing it to a fact
        rather than a fashion
    of construing or misconstruing the world

have always prevailed
        Sulpicius Severus (who recorded
    how Saint Martin after

his *guilty communion* with bishops
        in order to save a sinner
    felt a loss *of spiritual power*   *Sulp. Sev. Dial. 2.13; Hoare 137*

                                                                    37

a loss such as Gandhi felt)   *Kytle 173; P.D.Scott '89 116*
   later condemned by Augustine
  as a semi-Pelagian

for his belief it is not from genes
   or the fall of Eve
  that we have seen evil prevail

(much as Wang Yangming believed   *Pound Cantos 87/570*
   in the truth of original mind
  unselfish not beclouded)   *Wang Yangming; Chan 674*

but from *mala condotta*   *evil governance;*
a world ill-governed in our time   *Purgatorio 16.103*

II.v

Quick! first stack the plates
   pushed through the wicket window
  dump glasses dunk flatware

meat goes in can for the dog
   the rest into the garbage
  scour out enormous pots

I could have slept in as a child
   which don't even fit in the sink
  say *You're welcome!* to those

who peek through and say *Thanks!*
   maybe two hundred servings
  in the space of one hour

more near the end of the month
   when the homeless are waiting
  for their next welfare checks

I owe to Ronna
      this nostalgia of working hard
   one hour a week in the soup kitchen

at the McGee Avenue Baptist Church
      (it is years since I have used my hands
   like this though I remember

kitchen work somewhere in my youth
      the stoop labor in the tobacco fields)
   Or some days I take the names

as they come filing in
      I notice so many of them
   write their names left-handed

misfits who with my better luck
      might have become poets
   who have been joking some time outside

even when it is raining (though once
      Mack had to phone the police)
   when things are hopeless enough

you no longer have to worry!
      not by any means all black
   like the family of deaf-mutes

signing excitedly
      except when carrying their trays
   the blind Byron whom I

got to serve at table
      because he liked to talk about Byron
   and by then it had got around

I was an English teacher
      not just at a high school
   like Winston who sets out the forks

but at the university
          especially after Selma
     who helps serve vegetables

on the women's side of the kitchen
          (that is—next to the stove)
     and who has been to Europe

on a Berkeley Co-op travel package
          in one and the same week
     saw Ronna's *Glamour* magazine

piece on Dieters Feed the Hungry
          and me on TV
     and made much of this

after one of the prayer circles
          when for a minute we join hands
     asking the spirit to join us

and those outside we are about to feed
          I want all of you to know
     that our Ronna here

is DOCTOR Ronna Kabatznick
          Well! now it's my turn
     to tell all of you

Isaac who could never get me to slow down
          Betty the former cook
     at whose reception we served

after she got remarried
          to someone in the line
     Mack so silent the day

his son had been found dead
          Mrs. Harper whose granddaughter was murdered
     (you know about trials

all you women who spoke
        at Pearl's funeral
    about how you had moved together

from Richmond to Berkeley
        to worship at the same church)
    how grateful we are

not just because it is easier
        to walk through the heaps
    of seated bodies on the sidewalks

near the Automated Teller Machines
        much as Gibbon described them
    in his *Decline and Fall*

of the Roman Empire
        but because it is a privilege
    to encounter dignity

both of those in the line
        (the old lady in a knitted tam
    who chews so quietly

through three successive servings)
        but above all your dignity
    who organized this kitchen

for what you thought at first
        would be only one winter
    because *it was a job*

someone had to take care of
        for three years now
    you have come back day after day

addressing the suffering around you
        with the simplicity
    Eliot admired in Wordsworth

41

as *a profound spiritual revival*
          from trying *to imitate*
          and as far as possible to adopt

the very language of men   Eliot '34 74, 75, 80
          (what America like China wants
          a society where everyone

can read each other)
          In our city compounded
          from every continent

you have managed to maintain
          a simplicity which may not
          comprehend the world

but is able to heal it
          and thus able also
          to teach the rest of us

the task so straightforward
          we need only do it
          without raising any question

it has to be done

                    II.vi

They banished Solzhenitsyn to the West
          where he preached against détente
          and *the rot of Western life*

billboards and tabloids
          the lyrics of rock music
          the exploits of Daniel Ellsberg

"Freedom! to divulge
        the defense secrets of one's country
        for personal political gain"   *Remnick 70*

and because of *his* knowledge
        of Soviet defense secrets
        they imprisoned Sakharov at home

leaving Solzhenitsyn by default
        to exploit his reputation
        as *the dominant writer of this century*

causing the *nouveaux philosophes*
        like André Glucksmann
        to take *a strong anti-Communist stance*

and end *the spell of Jean-Paul Sartre*   *Remnick 70, 73*
        as well as encourage those
        inside and outside the Agency

who agreed that the U.S.
        was still *"being deceived*
        There are still P.O.W.s in Vietnam"   *Remnick 74*

whereas Sakharov could speak only
        in the quiet of his living room
        to people like you Dan   *Daniel Ellsberg*

leaving us to wonder
        what if the Cold War
        as you and Sakharov had wished

had ended in disarmament
        instead as Solzhenitsyn had wished
        being *"essentially won*

by Ronald Reagan when he embarked
        on the Star Wars program
        and the Soviet Union

could not take this next step"   Remnick 77
       Star Wars a response
  to the predictable finding of the B Team

that CIA Estimates
       had underestimated Soviet strength
       the United States had not prepared sufficiently   Ranelagh 623

relying on the dubious
       telemetry doublecross
  and *war of the moles*   Epstein '89 162-99, 260

a war not noticed by my colleagues
       who had marched so many times
  and been driven into hopeful

intensities of togetherness
       and high eloquence
  by the simplicities of Vietnam

As Plato once wrote
       you cannot be both powerful in the state
       and unlike it in character   Plato Gorgias 513B

but it was not just those wishing peace
       even Kissinger
  sent a memo to the White House

we recommend that the President
       not receive Solzhenitsyn   Remnick 72
  The net result of the clamor

coming partly from Helms's CIA
       and in a small way
  perhaps even from those of us

who wrote of *Nixon and the Mafia*   Weissman 251, 265, 270
       not knowing what dark forces
  were engaged in domestic battle

high over our civilian heads)
       the net result of all this
    was to bring down Nixon Kissinger

in the end William Colby
       thus opening up the way
    to Carter and Brzezinski

pushing through a decision
       to support the opium-growing
    Afghan rebels   *Scott and Marshall 178, 254; Brzezinski 427*

as well as Bush and the B Team
       the Bloomingdale Kitchen Cabinet
    General Graham's High Frontier   *Marshall Scott & Hunter 62, 76*

supported by Texas oilmen
       who from the early '80s
    were lusting after Central Asian oil

It would be wrong to
       derive some Manichaean moral
    there was no one evil strain

it having been the great
       Enlightenment failing
    to demonize church or class

No! I can agree like Havel
       with *some of Solzhenitsyn's obsessions*
    the need for a spiritual dimension

the need for the East
       to see capitalism and democracy
    with a clear eye   *Remnick 74-75*

his view of Yeltsin's mistake
       in appointing Gaidar
    a theorist under the influence

of the International Monetary Fund
        with *total ignorance*
        of the situation in Russia   *Remnick 78*

And despite his so-called
        poems in the English language
        which appear in every public place

I can agree with Brodsky
        (who inspired Susan Sontag to suggest
        that the *Reader's Digest*

had been more accurate than The Nation
        in its assessment of Communism)   *Remnick 73*
        that *Western man*

is a mental bourgeois
        who cherishes his mental comfort
        It is almost impossible for him

to admit disturbing evidence   *Remnick 73*
        one must admire both of them
        in a tyranny a real writer

is like a second government   *Remnick 79*
        their ability to stand up
        and push history back

even if in a wrong direction
        unlike the thinkers of the west
        using ghostly Marxist dialect

in their classroom wargames
        but if you Dan and Sakharov
        had been the ones who had been heard

and given us disarmament
        would we now have in Afghanistan
        the Hezb-i-Islami of Hekmatyar

the bombing of the World Trade Center
the slaughters in Sarajevo?

II.vii

Dukkha the first noble truth
            not just *suffering but imperfection*
      impermanence Buddhism itself

Rahula 17

decaying from insight
            to tradition and then
      in America new again

like the Christian churches
            having exhausted each other
      new-born in Korea and Japan

nothing ever its ideal
            the Peace Studies program
      which for my sins I helped start

was a pond of *dukkha*
            from which I escaped with my life
      Nothing is ever what was intended

certainly not a university
            strangled from the outset
      by sincere democratic committees

and you are lucky if you can sort out causes
            to explain why anything   the Court
      the Congress the press

has gone so terribly wrong
            Take a murderous fiasco
      like the Bay of Pigs

47

one must have compassion for the
                powerlessness of everyone
        Castro's paranoia

that led to the prison camps
                the response of the middle class
        flocking to Miami and pressuring

both presidential candidates
                to do something impossible
        a just and noble

restoration of freedom
                It's of course not this simple
        but even the CIA

caught between the law
                the political process
        its own trained executioners

and consumed by inner conflict
                between factions representing
        the legitimate claims

(and later grievances) of each
                must have seemed
        torrential *dukkha*

to those with the eyes to see it
                and for those more blind
        what they feared most

a great aching
                personal impotence   what I took away
        from my own four short years

in the service of a lesser power
                just that   the sense
        of general powerlessness

shared by those supposed to govern
        with private executives blocked
    by Lilliputian regulations

and reporting requirements
        Not that the alternative
    of those with the mindless faith

to impose their own vision
        investors who buy factories
    with no other motive

than to close them down
        or for a few brief years
    Pol Pot

dotting the fields of Cambodia
        with neat piles of skulls
    is any more hopeful

So without renouncing
        the age-old search
    for radical relief

of radical suffering
        I accept the process
    in which life ceases to be

like a movie with an ending
        and becomes a great *tanka*
    in which paradise hell

and above all *samsara*
        the cycle of continuous change
    even resurrection

an annual event
        are exhibited and experienced
    all at the same time

I hoped that poets
          might build fresh vantages
     more durable than bronze   *aere perennius; Horace Odes 3.30.1*

for this old vision
          but custom itself has a fate
     defiance of style

becomes subservience to it
          in less than a lifetime
     language itself is

not just a prime exhibit
          of ceaselessly changing *dukkha*
     (the Lord's Prayer still

my mantra though I now think about
          words like *father* and *kingdom*)
     but most important

language encodes our habit
          of defining others
     as the source of wrong

a habit that has involved
          the very best of us
     as co-conspirators

and makes *dukkha* survive

                    II.viii

I remember when very young
          canoeing with my father
     the St. Lawrence River in spate

below the Lachine Rapids
      how he emphasized the importance
   of paddling at first upstream

so as to be sure of getting back
      our frantic efforts
   to keep the canoe pointed straight

converted by a simple turn
      into effortless grace
   as we plied with inspiring speed

down past the flooded willows
      to my anxious mother
   The experience of history

was like a river
      into which like so many
   I was launched unawares

at first in the easy direction
      whatever we said or wrote about the war   *Vietnam War*
   reached with a strength

we thought mistakenly to be our own
      as when for example I answered
   in *The New York Review of Books*

McNamara's version of Tonkin Gulf   *New York Review 1/29/70*
      or Nixon's statement on Laos   *New York Review 4/9/70*
   with a blizzard of footnotes

which still amaze me
      collected not just by myself
   but from whole libraries of clippings

compiled by the movement
      after the Tet Offensive
   made it indelibly clear

(at least to the bankers)
> the war was a *costly error*   *Kolko '94 424; P.D.Scott '74 109–14*
> Even when the *New York Review*

stopped publishing essays
> by Chomsky and myself
> there was still the high elected

official of the State of California
> who came one Saturday to my office
> after I had written on Howard Hughes

and indicated by gestures
> we should only talk outside
> whose secretary thereafter

fed me with more leading questions
> about other politicians' involvement
> with Paul Ziffren

the lawyer from Chicago
> whose handling of the fortunes
> of those *who fronted*

for the Chicago mob's top hierarchy   *Demaris 242*
> I had already written about
> because of his involvement

with Jack Ruby's old mentor
> Jake Arvey (Ziffren's partner
> and the power behind Stevenson)   *Adlai Stevenson*

But just as I had declined
> after much vacillation
> to testify in Oslo

at the Bertrand Russell Tribunal
> after learning my airfare
> would be handled by Aeroflot

so I declined the material
        on Paul and Muriel Ziffren
    not relishing the standard role

of an *investigative journalist*
        with *inside sources*
    i.e. a catspaw to someone motivated

especially an elected politician
        who confided in me (when I talked
    of how the disposal of the Hale

family department store
        had helped Robert Vesco become rich)
    Oh yes

I was part of that deal!
        Depressed that my canoe
    was now pretty much dead in water

between the new mainstream
        of prisons and Star Wars
    and the sluggish side-current

of the Democratic Party
        drifting slowly backwards
    from the union liberalism of Ed Muskie

(whose California primary in '72
        had been managed by Paul Ziffren)
    to Carter the protégé

of CBS News and the CFR   *Council on Foreign Relations*
        I lost the energy
    to go deeper and learn why Maheu

after the CIA plots
        had the Hughes organization
    enjoying $6 billion in *secret*

non-competitive CIA contracts   P.D.Scott '77 29
          bought a Las Vegas casino
     from his friend Moe Dalitz

of the old Cleveland syndicate
          (with even a finder's fee
     for Johnny Roselli the mobster

before he was murdered)   P.D.Scott '77 29
          or to learn why Karen's boyfriend   P.D.Scott '89 107
     when they slept in the VIP suite

at a Reno hotel
          said *we even do business*
     with the University of California

impenetrable mysteries!
          where once I had believed
     that knowledge conferred power

at last mindful of wife and children
          and one or two murdered friends
     I retreated to dry land

to deal with the written world
          letting others strengthen the hope
     that through understanding

of the darkness around us
          we can move towards freedom
     That we may see the Open!   dass wir das Offene schauen

both by day and by night   Hölderlin '52 146
          (As a friend has observed
     we cannot claim we have mastered

the secret of the world
          by our power to blow it up)   Hegel '75A 71; MacGregor '98 28
     In my dream of no water

54

the path through the cave
          curved around and upward
     towards the hint of light

the source above the rapids
          to reach which one
     must forget the canoe

while if we drift
          the other way downstream
     the river will slowly widen

into a catastrophe
          where life no longer appears
     as a landscape of objects

or even a river
          but as an open end
     against a darkness

of no naming

II.ix

Our ancestors were pirates
          (Thucydides admitted) but now   *Thucydides 1.1*
     we have seen over four centuries

the steady flow of so much wealth
          from the poor nations to the richest
     is it too late to ask

(along with my mother   descended
          from Maccus the Viking
     the predator Lairds of Carlaverock)

that since this wealth dissolves
        the painfully established
    communities we have grown accustomed to

of Athens (this collapse
        took less than a century)
    Florence Spain England

and now the United States   *Marshall Scott & Hunter 227–29*
        can we not now dedicate
    policy to nobler goals

than maximizing wealth?
        Like maybe a polis
    at peace with itself

where men and women can walk safely
        on their streets at night?
    It is as if the sudden

collapse of the Soviet Union
        had robbed us of our future   *MacGregor '98 142*
    Why cannot economists

who micromanage the arbitrage
        of dollars in the markets
    of London Singapore and Hong Kong

why cannot they plan
        instead of increasing GNP
    to shrink the costly gap

costly to every one of us
        between the rich and the poor?
    If we still talk of sovereignty

and even freedom   could we not
        in this year of jubilee   *Leviticus 25:10-13*
    take this step to correct history

(a step closer and more important
          than walking on the moon)?
     And since we know

this is not about to happen
          let us give one reason why
     poetry (the *more philosophic*

version of truth)   Aristotle Poetics 9.2
          has given place to fiction
     the random moment

comparatively independent
          of the unstable orders
     over which men fight and despair   *Auerbach '57 488*

the novels which at first
          helped energize the middle class
     now help to sedate them

Weltliteratur which first
          helped bring the world together
     now serves to isolate us

the only time I ever
          managed to shock an audience
     one that thought itself quite comfortable

with blasphemies against God
          was when I said
     right into the microphone

I prefer truth to fiction
          and the world might be better off
     if we read more truth   less fiction

and for the first time
          at that whole conference
     no one spoke to me afterwards

But could they handle truth?
　　　　it is not fun to read Chomsky
　　　Wilson's troops murdered destroyed　　　　　　　*Woodrow Wilson*

reinstituted virtual slavery　　　　　　　　　　　*Chomsky '93 202*
　　　　to be continuously
　　reminded we are still pirates

exporting our freedom to consume
　　　　which not only dissatisfies
　　(Shirine's grandmother *was distraught*

when Reza Shah Pahlavi
　　　　forbade women to wear the veil
　　and commanded them

to be European in appearance　　　　　　　　　*Klein 62*
　　　　but impoverishes the many
　　and as for the few

wealthy enough
　　　　to be pure consumers of fiction
　　they *eat of the lotus*

and forget their homeward way　　　　　　　　*Odyssey 9.102*

II.x

Good Friday! I lie in bed
　　　　in a millennial mood
　　without a heart to choose

between those who in the name
　　　　of enlightenment and peace
　　have thrown off all restraints

from ritual and text
        (*Kant's rigorous distinction*
    leaving *the hereafter*

emptied of *this world*   *Lilla 38*
    and ourselves *transported*
    toward a "cataract")   *Benjamin '95; Lilla 39*

and those who now revive
        old memories of hate
    of jihad and crusade

Tempted to reprove
        both sides for having lost
    dialogue with the voices

of sanity in the past
        I am minded to go back
    for the first time in two decades

and celebrate Easter
        in the church across the street
    (returning to that glimpse

I had of a new life
        which once drew me to pray
    in the snow and jonquils

of La Pierre Qui Vire   *Benedictine monastery*
        just as the earth itself
    by Dante's calculus

now returns to its first point
        in the *ordo saeclorum*)   *Inferno 1.38-40;*
    except that in this year   *Virgil Ecl. 4.5*

by an arcane computation
        of progress and return
    Easter and Pesach coincide   *Passover*

This year I will choose Pesach
        and in truth as a Christian
just because both religions

bring us to atonement
        I prefer this time to hear
in the Pesach service

the never silenced phrases
        of Israel *out from Egypt*   *Psalm 114:1*
the song of Dante's pilgrims   *Purgatorio 2.47*

a message from the past
        that tells of liberation
within not just outside

the linear course of time
        and projects it forward
You were aliens in Egypt

you shall not oppress an alien   *Exodus 23:9*
        Why should I not feel guilt
(the keynote of this age

echo of bloodstained madness)   *Benjamin '78 256*
        having read because of Ronna
how in this Easter week

of the year 1264
        (and its blood-libel rumor
of the young Hugh of Lincoln

crudeliter crucifixus   *Walsingham ad ann. 1255*
        or *slayn with cursed Jewes*   *Chaucer 164*
as recalled for English Lit

by Chaucer's prioresse
        with her *tendre herte*)   *Chaucer 18*
a number of London Jews

estimated at hundreds
> were killed on the eve of Pesach
> the customary date?   *Roth 61–62; Sachar 199*

We can't just blame the rabble
> even the Church's Fathers
> like Saint John Chrysostom

attacked *the Synagogue*
> as *a whorehouse and den of thieves*   *Adv. Iudaeos 1.3*
> Saint Ambrose the patrician

in response to the burning
> by Christians of a synagogue
> *a receptacle of folly*

which God Himself has condemned
> rebuked not the culprits
> but the punishing emperor   *Ambrose Epistola 40; Patrologia Latina 16.1103*

So Ronna I might convert
> had I not this need to stay
> with the sins of my fathers

or is this an excuse
> it having been my style
> always to be withholding

at the edge of commitment
> just as you and I
> will continue to chant

the Buddhist refuges
> and find in meditation
> an approach to nothingness

like that of Simone Weil
> who teetering on the edge
> between Jewish and Christian

wrote *the perfection*
        of the spiritual life
    is to consent to be nothing   *Weil '63 30*

Should I rebuke myself
        for always celebrating
    as a green card alien

or is this a necessary
        atonement for self and world
    where as Augustine said   *civis sursum, peregrini deorsum*

by grace we are aliens   *Augustine City of God 15.1*
        from the time of Jesus' death
    to Strasbourg *on the Sabbath*

eighteen hundred Jews
        dragged and burnt alive   *Sachar 201*
    after which Luther

Burn down their synagogues
        drive them out like mad dogs   *Luther 292*
    and in this final age

the Easter massacres
        unleashed by fearful tsars
    with the same blood-libel rumor   *Sachar 320-22*

found in America   *Dundes 233-42*
        I think of how World War Two
    eclipsed my father's vision

of enlightenment and law
        and roused him to new gloom
    Christ in the darkness dead

his hope for man too soon
        sealed with the outer stone   *F.R. Scott 190*
    and feel myself succumb

to that acerbic rhythm
        which sees all fates as one
    death and liberation

the ritual demise
        of Pharaoh in the flood
    and of the Second Temple

with its animal sacrifice
        of Baghdad in its prime
    and then avenging Rome

passionate to defend
        the Bible with the sword
    and now of the holy cities

of Shi'ite Chechen Kurd
        bombed by secular powers
    fearful of revenge

from the God-fearing gangs
        roving their capitals
    the vision beyond reach

becomes the grave of each   *F.R. Scott 190*
        wrote my father during war
    his rationalistic mentors

yielding one by one
        to the return of the repressed
    Freud having once dismissed

The Future of an Illusion
        returned to his fathers' faith
    in *Moses and Monotheism*

like the atheist H.G. Wells
        the end is close at hand   *Wells '46 1*
    that congruence of mind

attributed   by *man*
     to the secular process
   not really there at all   *Wells '46 3*

and those not trapped in reason
     ventured like Benjamin
    that amid the destruction

we would meet an angel   *Benjamin '78 273*
     All this had to happen
    time is a hologram

transcending repetition
     by the power from despair
    to emancipate *quotations*

from their *demeaning bondage*   *Benjamin '78 xxxvi*
     that power which is the grace
    to recognize *the thing*

we believe to be ourself
     as a product of circumstance   *Weil '77 458*
    time haunted now as then

by the continuous ghost
     of another dimension
    both there and yet not there

discovering liberation
     not just in release from time
    but in the *ordo saeclorum*   *Virgil Ecl. 4.5*

and not just in the end of time
     (that millennial Easter
    when God shall be all in all)   *1 Cor. 15:28;*
                                 Milton Paradise Lost 3.341

but in this jubilee year   *2000 C.E.*
     which should be for us as for Dante   *1300 C.E.*
    a year of forgiveness   *Purgatorio 2.98–99*

to proclaim liberty   *Leviticus 25:10*
    you shall not sow nor reap
  but shall return everyone

unto his possession   *Leviticus 25:11-13; cf. Virgil Ecl. 4.40-41*

II.xi

And am I to reenact
    the intellectualizations
  and didactic commonplaces

(*many errors*
    a little rightness)   *Pound Cantos 116/797*
  of old men's *Paradisos*?

To abandon the *tohu-bohu*   *utter confusion; Gen. 1:2*
    of destructive creation
  the Apollonian promise

of the Fourth Eclogue   *Virgil Ecl. 4.10*
    to rise from our *worm-like state*
  and spread abroad

the wings of Liberty   *Prelude 10.836-37*
    out of disappointment
  self-recrimination

and sheer loss of nerve?
    Perilous is sweeping change   *Wordsworth '81 2.819*
  All things are best fulfilled

in their due time   *Milton Paradise Regained 3.182*
    Milton's *Readie and Easie Way*
  to Establish a Free Commonwealth

ignored (*these words are simple*
            no one can practice them)   *Tao Te Ching 70*
    by the crowds already preparing

(*in the general depravity*
        of the human mind)   *Milton 389*
    to cheer the king's return

just as Dante cursing
        the *wicked and senseless*   *Paradiso 17.62*
    made a virtue of having been

a party unto yourself   *Paradiso 17.68-69*
        after losing faith in change
        (one cannot rectify the world

before she is ready)   *Paradiso 30.138*
        Both success and failure
    make it hard to question oneself

(as the archer missing the target
        seeks the cause in himself)   *Confucius Zhongyong 15.4;*
    to recall the ancient poems   *Legge 396; Cantos 77/468*

read early with rapture
        in a college garden
        (the dazzling paradisal light

warblers darting in the lilacs)
        and deal with the temptation
    to heighten one's closure

and thus ring false
        or take refuge in easy
    complacencies: that America

however fallible was better
        when its leaders like John Adams
    were schooled in Plato and Cleanthes

and *wrote on Greek prosody* Cantos 71/420; Adams '56 10.265
for which decline we should blame
not so much the electorate

as our structural aging
into compartmentalization
above all in our universities

(*the social sciences*
without the humanities
are not scientific

the humanities
without the social sciences
are not humane)

the requirement for our neglected
policies of slaughter:
the enforced separation

of political from moral sense
Oxford and Cambridge
rejecting their heritage

when they burned their Platonic books
as *Popish or diabolical*   *Wood 1.89; 2.107; French 27*
turned to Ciceronianism   *Sidney 132; French 27*

or as we now call it
language philosophy
"the chiefe abuse"   *mere words*   *Sidney 132; French 27*

and thus to the desert inside the Beltway
that has forced in turn the creation
of those smaller groups

that will survive
because they reward the heart
a third millennium of NGOs   *Non-Governmental Organizations*

67

open　　　*egalitarian*　　　　　　　　　*Habermas '96 366*
　　　floating like plankton in cyberspace
　　from East Timor to Brazil

in the struggle (as Milton
　　　　attempted to English it)
　　　to debel the proud　　　　　　　*Milton Paradise Regained 4.305;*
Aeneid 6.853

a struggle determined
　　　　by the test of love
　　what will remain

in another thousand years
　　　　　returned to each nighttime
　　two sweet skulls

breathing closely together
two sweet skeletons entwined

II.xii

I tell my mother
　　　　who now can hardly talk
　　why I am late this morning

the long quiet in bed
　　　　after this big dream:
　　It was the anniversary

of some great counter-culture
　　　　event like Woodstock
　　thousands of us walked up early

into wilderness
　　　　to arrange bedding for the night
　　comfortable with just a sleeping bag

alone I shared with a stranger
          one floor of an abandoned semi-Victorian
     farmhouse the one old structure

waiting for some event   But there was only
          the arrival of more and more people
     no organizers of the free concert

It was all very well for me to say
          last week on a radio program
     that the left in the sixties

was wrong to polarize
          this nation into conflict
     now I think we could not have had

that frenetic organization of detail
          without some mean American
     competitiveness I have never grown used to

no free music no turf on the streets
          no half-naked women dancing
     on the back of a flatbed truck

but then what in the end did all that achieve
          other than elect Reagan
     and reveal the state's incompetent

brutality when people
          were roused to act against it?
     Anyhow the crowd in my dream became so great

I did nothing but say to strangers
          No! This place is saved
     and later when whole families

at least two mothers with small children
          were poking around I thought it better
     to let two or three of them in

as a protection against the rest
        though the truth was there was no protection
    it was hard to show occupancy

with just a sleeping bag and a spare shirt
        and about this time someone with a pole
    smashed my window and began to jab openings

in the flimsy shingles
        methodically all around the house
    a deliberated pattern

like the misshapen dwarf I remember
        from the last seventies tear gas
    with no arms or hands to speak of

trying to break the plate glass window
        of some innocent watchmaker
    with his leather-sheathed head

I did not know whether to cry out
        or to pretend I was not there inside
    there being so little legitimacy

in acting like a bourgeois
        I apologize to my mother
    for this dream *this is what comes*

from reading you the later Yeats
        who so feared the modern tide
    of *formless, spawning, fury*   Yeats '89 337

or maybe because today
        as I putter in the kitchen
    again protected by my customs

of breakfast tea and bread
        is just two years since the fire
    when I sat with the chickadees

unable to think of nature
        as the pelican finding food
    for its blind mate

or as history's strain
        to come back to gentleness
    But my mother the yea-sayer

in the midst of her striving
        to shake free from life
    still strong with faith

that with hearts in the right joy
        of experience we gain
    more from life than we can lose

able today to speak
        in the barest whisper says *no!*
    it is the fantasy you can dare

voice and expel from yourself
        knowing that you are
    no longer alone since Ronna

has left on your pillow last night
        the letter you just read to me
    her wanting "to cry

from the sheer pleasure and depth
        of love"
    the letter signed

"your wife"

FIRST RETREAT:
FIRE-TENDING IN THE LAND OF MEDICINE BUDDHA

For Gil Fronsdal and Tamara Kan

1
BREATH

I focus on breath
and at the same time

on keeping an even fire
the draft so the log will catch

the damper to bring the roar
down to a murmur

much like my own breath
I see the blue smoke

beyond the window
rise through treetops

in the redwood canyon
it is hard to focus

on not thinking
when I see the jackets

of the silent sitters
slowly unbuttoned

I have made them comfortable
the smoke a reassuring ribbon

till my mood is broken
by the teacher I hoped to please

Too warm!
I want to see them

wrapped up in their blankets

2

seeing one's whole life
linked by the fires

one time or another one has lit
half-way up a mountain

or by the luminous ocean
breathing all night

is like seeing this continent
from a jet-liner

the third of a century
crammed into a career

now shrunk to a small
urban smudge

in the magnificent green hills

3
BODY (*KAYA*)

grateful to have
these four channels

inward from eyes and ears
this human windpipe

this diaphragm
that takes care of breathing

the comfort of support
at the small of the back

this stomach full
of warm oatmeal

I am willing to forgive
these wretched unbending

Western knees

4

the breathing fire
a meditation

the right level of flames
already lost

the teacher just now
saying *to remove*

fuel for your thoughts
I think of Jacopone da Todi

incandescent
with the love of God

conflagration
and attempt to return

my mind to *focus*
which meant originally

hearth

5

the silence
of sitting together

(even with total strangers
one has never talked to)

so much closer than speech
as I learned well

in those six months
watching my mother

slowly fulfil her resolution
to die

6

FEELINGS (*VEDANA*)

may my heart
like this creaky stove-pipe

expand softly
to its own music

give off gentle warmth
not smoke

7

by the fourth day
I have learnt to watch how wide

is the rivulet of air
around the stove pipe

in which the window-sill quivers
the buckeye branches swim

on the altar
are two red crystal goblets

is it too much to think
one could keep the highlight

in the closer one
twinkling from time to time

the further one calm?

8

MENTAL STATES (*CITTA*)

sparks inside the stove
startling the darkness
so many fires

my parents sprinkling magic
from crystals and *papiers d'Arménie*

fragrant yucca-stem and sage
on a hill above Tassajara

—*note digression digression*

the sound of my breath
in front of our tarpaulin
dry balsam crackling through the rain

flames under the auditorium door
as (according to the *Chronicle*)
I led my students out of Wheeler Hall

—*ego is thinking this*

note that my feet are cold
the providential warm hut
that saved us in the mountain white-out

—*important to keep calm*

when we tried to find our house
and sneaked past the police barrier
at four that next morning

we saw yet another home
in the abandoned pine trees

—*no stopping this*

smoulder neglectedly
and begin to burn

9

walking almost in place
lifting moving falling

as the phantom
redwoods and gompa   *meditation hall*

hobble slowly toward us
a world of fog all around

in which chickadees
chirp here and there

like stars

10

beyond the edge
of the Enchanted Forest

the trail marked *No Entrance*
becomes a logging road

on to a hillside
where they are cutting down redwoods

to pay for the campaign
to save Tibet

11
DHAMMA

expand from this breathing
towards contented fire

gentle sobbing to my right
to which I once again

send out my red mental
child's firetruck of *metta*   *loving-kindness*

under the awning
of expanded presence

lifted higher by a passing plane
appear unasked-for images

the hollow redwood
with a fire-glow inside it

the man-sized pelican
in the logging road

the *papier maché*
head of a loved one

on a plate at the back of the stove
can be let go of

the pure white light
next to me on my left

especially when I peek
the effigy of an ancient

white hawk-god
just my height standing

begins to endure

12

the mindfulness
of fire-tending

taught me by my father
the importance

of not resorting to paper
how in a rainstorm

to split softwood with an axe
and kindle with splinters

from the tree's core
or with a penknife

to whittle dead twigs
for their inner shavings

how birchbark
will burn when wet

the secret
inner heart

of that public man

13

what lasts?
the streak

of the brown dipper
flying up the streambed

already gone

14

fifty of us
in silent single file

up through the meadow
past the noble stump

with the oblong hole
carved by its executioner

and silver filigree
from thousands of bark beetles

to the green shades
of the Enchanted Forest

may this joy I have met
sunbeams mists

wet eyelids
of redwood branches

remain in place
for those behind me

who have been in pain

each of us gives a turn
to the Tibetan prayer wheel

as we at the front
come down around the bend

the bell rings
fainter and fainter

the last ringers behind us
can barely be heard

through the increasingly loud
trudging

of freshly wet gravel

III

YIN

"The Tao that enlightens appears dark"   *—Tao Te Ching 41*

"I seek a unity all-pervading"   —Confucius, *Analects* 15.2.3

"Wisdom is one thing: to understand the intelligence which steers all through all things."   —Heraclitus, fragment 41

"My heart has become capable of every form: it is a pasture for
    gazelles
and a convent for Christian monks, and a temple for idols, and
    the
pilgrim's Ka'ba, and the tables of the Torah and the book of
    the Qur'an.
I follow the religion of Love, whichever way His camels take."
                                          —Ibn 'Arabi

        "poets, even as prophets, each with each
Connected in a mighty scheme of truth"
                      —Wordsworth, *Prelude* 12.301–02

III.i

Nietzsche described *the struggle*
    against the Dionysiac *Nietzsche '67 82; Snell 120*
the Apollonian Socrates

destroying the ancient culture
    by seeking to understand it
stripping the tragic art

of all things noble *Aristophanes Frogs 1494-95;*
Snell 113
    in the name of knowledge
but in *The Discovery of the Mind*

(which might for another author
    have been *Mind Discovering Itself*)
Snell equilibrates this contrast

seeing *Socratic "knowledge"*
    the element of reflexion
at the birth of tragedy

as well as *at its demise* *Snell 122*
    In Homer a man is unaware
of his own volition *Snell 123*

when a *thought comes* from without *Snell 31, 123*
    in the form of Athene
to the irate Achilles *Iliad 1.206-13*

the hero acts with *perfect assurance*
    not *burdened with scruples* *Snell 123*
whereas Orestes in Aeschylus

caught between two divine commands
    must choose for himself
    in *a proud awareness of his freedom*   *Snell 123*

For Snell it is *the Greeks*
    who *discovered the human mind*   *Snell vii*
    and thus founded our civilization   *Snell 31–32*

Goethe shines through Snell's pages   *Snell 135, etc.*
    Those closest to the god
    are the strong and powerful   *Snell 33*

Darkness and death have been pushed
    to the farthest limits   *Snell 34*
    the gods large and beautiful

as once in Wagner's Valhalla
    until in the first Attic tragedy
    the dark forces regain their power

and the terror of the mysterious
    asserts itself once more   *Snell 37*
    For Snell it *is not Greek*

to believe what is absurd   *Snell 29*
    (For *a Greek the bargaining*
    between Gideon and his God   *Judges 6:36-40*

would be *more than a little peculiar*)   *Snell 28*
    Snell does not consider
    whether in the Bible

mind was also discovering itself
    Xenophanes' *most fruitful discovery*
    "There is one god"   *Xenophanes fr. 23*

makes him for Snell the first
    to have a revelation of the divine
    as a comprehensive unity   *Snell 141*

forgetting the *Shema* in the Torah
　　　the Lord is one *Deut. 6:4*
　　Admittedly it is easier

to raise this matter in Berkeley
　　　than for Snell in Hamburg
　　in the year 1942

when his disparagement of cult
　　　and myth in the name of freedom
　　had some local urgency

as a challenge to the Nazis
　　　but the real problem was Goethe
　　the discoverer of *Historismus* *Auerbach '57 394*

and hence of *Weltliteratur* *Auerbach '69*
　　　one of the very last
　　to seek that oxymoron

an enlightened ruler
　　　It took Auerbach to see
　　that the limitations of Homer

life is enacted
　　　only among the ruling class
　　nothing ever pushes up from below *Auerbach '57 18*

are exactly reflected in Goethe
　　　for whom *the fulfillment*
　　of beautiful possibilities

lies entirely in the flowering
　　　of aristocratic cultures
　　this explains *his aversion*

to the explosive and violent
　　　recalcitrant masses *Auerbach '57 395*
　　Thus Snell's equilibrium

in his defense of enlightenment
                and his critique of Nietzsche's
        attack on *decadent style*   *Snell 134*

seem less at the heart
                of our western civilization   *Snell 32*
        than Auerbach's contrast

between Homer's discursive style
                and that of the Torah
        rätselvoll und hintergründig

(*mysterious and fraught-with-background*)   *Auerbach '57 9*
        perhaps to understand
        the civilization we are talking about

one must move beyond it?
                Snell wrote in the 1940s
        while teaching at Hamburg

and Auerbach in 1942
                began *Mimesis*
        ridiculously ambitious

an act of cultural survival
                of the highest importance   *Said '83 6; Said '93 47*
        from *the agonizing distance*   *Said '83 8*

of Turkey where *the libraries*
                are not well equipped
                for European studies   *Auerbach '57 492, Said '83 5*

and he was a refugee

III.ii

For Marian Dale Scott (June 26, 1906-November 28, 1993)

In my mother's studio
        I was not allowed to enter
    even when I was sixty-four

and she bedridden
        the easel still stood
    crusted with paint

(and still breathing it seemed to me
        the smells of turpentine
    shellac

although after the war
        she had shifted over
    from oil to acrylic)

an impasto thicker
        than Jackson Pollock's
    flecking even the walls and floor

when we sold off the house
        there being no money
    to make it a museum

a jolt to my earlier assurance
        that her art would endure
    My mother when eleven

had been part of the Spring Exhibition
        at the Montreal Museum of Fine Arts
    and thereafter pursued with attention

my father and I never mustered
        the *one thing needful*   *Luke 10:42*
    though she never finished high school

(one of my father's tics
        was to poke fun at her spelling)   *Please nock!*
    she loved George Eliot

and liked to quote Nietzsche
        Live dangerously!
        Count every day lost

that you have not danced!
        as well as Goethe
        not a circle

a spiral   *cf. Trépanier 130, 132*
        Despite her interest
    in pure patterns from science

Atom Bone and Embryo   *Trépanier 170-71*
        she seemed a little removed
    from the external world

it was by general agreement
        that she gave up driving
        and on her one fishing trip

her first and only trout
        still wriggling vigorously
    landed inside her blouse

But the more she receded
        from the details of this world
        the more she saw it whole

and my father generously admitted
        that of the two she seemed
    more serious about life

above all about inner life
        it was she who embarrassed me mornings
        did you have any dreams?

taught me to see   the beating wings
      of the yellow swallowtail
   in the purple lantanas

and led me to other seers
      of the everyday world
   Lismer   white-tonsured

his eagle eye looking out
      over us children
   still framing the space beyond us

with the clear air
      of a granite lake and wind-blown
   pine trees behind it

and of the inner world
      Borduas painting
   the pure act of painting itself

encouraging my young imagination
      to go beyond sense
   the more outrageously grotesque

my swiftly-drawn caricatures
      the more certain I felt
   of earning my mother's approval

Later I came to honor
      her search for a uniqueness
   leaving little space for enemies

her strength to respond
      to news of setback or betrayal
   not with personal recrimination

but with rededication to her art
      which left her less and less interest
   in the distractions of mere fame

I began to imitate
        her days of patient responses
    to inner guidance

(in her notebook   Kandinsky
        the artist must search deeply
    into his soul

develop and tend it
        so that his art does not remain
    a glove without a hand   *Trépanier 109 n.41*

from a world beyond sense
        (like Dante's *high phantasy*
    moved *when the senses offer nothing*)   *Purgatorio 17.16,25*

When we cleaned out the house
        I gave the easel
    along with the tall cupboards

to my cousin and godson Peter Collie
        and his wife Stéphanie the painter
    now they have moved to Australia

nothing is promised to endure
        not even this red sky
    she painted in the months

after my father died
        with two blue orbs and a broad
    volcanic flow of pigment

any more than this photo taken
        when my mother was eighty-two
    by the next-door neighbor

a Jewish woman who emigrated
        from North Africa in the sixties
    the first neighbor in forty years

who knew my mother at all
        It sits four feet away on my desk
    and catches my mother's face

but not her eyes
still looking behind me

                    III.iii

Although it is some time now
            since a god or goddess
        has fixed us eyeball to eyeball

the cosmologists return
            to talk of events inspired
        through hyperdimensional space

how *"extreme black holes"*
            in the original
        ten-dimensional universe

would behave like
            subatomic particles
        This sort of research

is of considerable interest
            since if string theory is right
        about everything's being made

of tiny strings of compressed
            [and hyperdimensional] space
        then subatomic particles are

in effect miniature
            black holes   *Ferris 49*
        They recall Poe's *Eureka*

91

denounced as the nonsensical
    product of a mind
  warped by opprobrium

opium and alcohol
    which portrayed the cosmos
  as an evolutionary system

built on hyperdimensional geometry
    The cosmologist Sandage
  seeking to break

the closed loop
    of induction-deduction
  mentions Poe's "*Eureka*"   *Ferris 50*

which *dismissed the methods*
    of both Bacon and Aristotle
  and *argued for a third method*

which he called imagination
    we now call it intuition   *Ferris 50*
  I in my epic classes

used to call it
    the right relationship to the gods
  granted to Achilles

when by listening to Athene
    he stayed his anger   *Iliad 1.214-17; Snell 155*
  but denied to Agamemnon

when he awoke from sleep
    and obeyed his baneful dream   *Iliad 2.41*
  methodless insight

from *successive iterations*   *Ferris 50*
    (Odysseus in the storm
  having pondered *in his mind and heart*   *Odyssey 5.365*

92

decided to disobey the goddess
        and do *what seemed the best*   *Odyssey 5.360*
    to stick with the raft while it endured

and then to swim
        seeing that there was *nothing better*
    to come up with)   *Odyssey 5.364*

until mind *eventually conforms*
        to nature   *Ferris 50*
    (when the wave

broke down upon him
        Odysseus as commanded
    put on the goddess' veil)   *Odyssey 5.356-64,373*

I am as heartened
        by reading the *New Yorker*
    in this night of insomnia

slaughter in Rwanda
        and McNamara's lies
    as when my peace of mind

which I almost lost
        in my junior year
    abandoning physics and mathematics

for the doubts of philosophy
        was restored by reading Whitehead's
    account of how Newton's

dogmatic system
        was enlarged by the prehensive
    intuitions of Wordsworth   *Whitehead 116–18*

I must send a letter to Gil
        who recalled his childhood daydream
    of a universe in each atom

much like my own dream
    a galaxy
into *a dot of pollen*   *P.D.Scott '92 92–93*

subatomic particles
    in effect black holes   *Ferris 49*
or *man in the Zohar*

the likeness
    that includes all likenesses   *Scholem 153*
the *macrocosm*   *microcosm*

of John Dee and Robert Fludd   *Yates 38, 52*
    John Dee the *magician who inspired*
the Elizabethan technical advance

the more mystical side of whose thought
    inspired Sidney and his circle
and the Elizabethan poetic movement   *Yates 221; Heilbron 48–49*

much as Guillaume Postel
    the Christian Kabbalist
inspired the Pléiade

who believed that *measured verse*
    would lead to a initiation
into a higher realm   *French 132–34*

and in whose Renaissance
    all Enlightenments
outer and inner   were one

cosmography a science
    of intellectual discovery
they thought Oriental wisdom might reveal

a concordia mundi   *French 181*
    a religious philosophy promising
a new dawn for mankind   *Yates 38*

detected in Isaac Newton   *Yates 220; cf. Heilbron 39*
          Sandage: *Simply start*
     like Poe trust

in the imagination
               (the book failed to sell out
     its initial press run

of five hundred copies)   *Ferris 50*
          which is more than fiction
     when it returns to dreams

(even Descartes' *cogito*
          the birth and bane of Enlightenment
     appeared to him in a dream)   *Seabrook 65*

and makes new dreams in turn
               imaginary negatives
     by night the constellations

of lupines on the hillside
by day the orchards of the stars

III.iv

Despite my good excuse
          (*You must vacate your office*
     by May 15th

this is a final notice)
          I cannot sleep
     with this distaste in my stomach

for the new me
          that has just sold off the old
     for 450 dollars

my vellum-bound *Civitas Dei*   *Augustine City of God*
        my troubadour poets in Provençal
    my two Icelandic dictionaries

that were like extensions of my brain
        in this office I once thought of
    as a home of dreams

I hear the rain flail
        the roof as if in displeasure
    at this treachery

the wind chime hectic
        as when I gave away
    to distant relatives and strangers

the heavy furniture of my mother's house
        we had lived in for five decades
    the brass bed that rattled

with my first tremulous pubescence
        the *death chair* of studded red leather
    where a great-great uncle died

though it is twelve years
        since I have lectured on the sagas
    the conversion of epic violence

birsirkir biting their swords   *berserk warriors*
        and *howling like dogs*   *Grettissaga xix*
    (the class always laughed at this)

into the familiar
        frustrations we know all about
    under a rule of law

the hero now outlaw
        þykkjumikill   (tending toward discord)
    in a society much like ours

only democratic
        until it was dulled
    by the same cooling climate

that expelled the Anasazi
        from the Canyon de Chelly
    the descending glaciers

I now feel *at my back*
        however gloriously they shone
    when I looked down on them

with a glass of champagne
        on my way home to San Francisco
    from the East Timor Symposium

at the University of Lisbon
        It is silly to pretend
    I will write as hoped

on that Icelandic classlessness
        compared to the Homeric kings
    our civilization looks back to

whose idea of love
        was to drive out the inhabitants
    from one of their own cities

to make space for a friend   *Odyssey 4.174-80*
        This is I guess my job now
    to throw away all false

illusions of possibility
        and attachments to past life
    manuscripts I shall never finish

on the emergence of freedom
        through refinements of metaphor
    along with the poster of Ho Chi Minh

whose eyes and mouth
        some unknown night-visitor
    slashed with a razor

arm-bands from forgotten vigils
        where we grouped nonviolently
    round raging provocateurs

the unexploded canister
        of CS gas
    the can of rations thrown in the grass

that year of bayonets
        by some disgusted
    kid in the National Guard

the yellowing manifestos
        for marches with garlands
    and gifted street music

whose promise of revolution
        was heard so widely
    that the people rose up

in unprecedented numbers
        and elected Governor Reagan
    we were *on the verge*

of something which seemed then
        altogether new
    and now—memorabilia

not much different from my father's
        when he cleaned out his office
    with his mementos of the Nile

his oar from Magdalen College
        (for rowing head of the river)
    stared at by the silent

heads of Buddha and Dante F.R.Scott 218
>> one cannot step twice
> into the same river

in which we discard our dreams
>> to drift downwards like corpses
> towards Les Alyscamps

dove Rodano stagna *where the Rhone is at rest;*
>> towards that land
> where poets talk together *Inferno 9.112*

in *the language of the sun*
>> of *life made pure through art* *Aeneid 6.662*
> which as the rains darken

the wet untasted millet
>> and pinewood of my birdfeeder
> appears to have been left

irreparably behind us

III.v

For Fay Stender, d. May 20, 1980

As we gaze through the window
>> at the unexpected hailstorm
> Marvin the host and I *Marvin Stender*

first introduced by our children
>> in nursery school
> now celebrate his grandchildren

Neal's two small daughters half-Chinese
>> here for Pesach from Hong Kong *Passover*
> paraded and touched like the Torah

by the admiring guests
          some old white-haired friends
     I do not recognize

some once at school with Cassie
          The food laid on by Dru
     Marvin's second wife

is sumptuous   but it is hard
          as I remark to Sandy
     when we leave together

sharing an umbrella
          not to feel at this party
     the presence of a ghost

the unmentioned Fay   *Fay Stender*
          who made the decision
     to *get out of the Prison Movement*

and give *all my attention to my body*
          as she told me twice
     the first time sunning by the pool

her swimsuit matching Oriane's
          mother and daughter like two mermaid sisters
     the second time two nights before the shooting

at a left-wing benefit dinner
          in San Francisco Chinatown
     when she could still talk of nothing else

I want to give all my attention to my body
          she said studying her hands
     which when she was fourteen

had played the "Emperor" concerto
          with the San Francisco Symphony   *Collier and Horowitz 25*
     I think if I were to lose my body health

I would want to die and two nights later
     the doorbell rang after midnight
  her son Neal answered

found a .38-caliber pistol in his face
     as the gunman pushed by him to find Fay
  told her she had betrayed the prison movement

then shot her five times *in the chest*
     abdomen and both arms   *Collier and Horowitz 55*
  she was left paralyzed

hiding out with a watchdog
     in unremitting pain
  which she endured as she had promised friends

until a year later when Sandy
     drove her to the airport
  she flew to Hong Kong

and ended her life   *Collier and Horowitz 65*
     David Horowitz angered
  almost all his old Berkeley friends

when he wrote how Fay like other
     left-wing women attorneys
  got too involved with her clients   *Collier and Horowitz 31*

was too willing to overlook
     the crimes of those she defended   *Collier and Horowitz 37*
  his reproof from his own pain

when the young white woman accountant
     for whom he had gotten the job
  of bookkeeping for the Black Panthers

came across something and was killed   *Collier and Horowitz 270, 295*
     Most people discounted David
  after he became a star

for the John M. Olin Foundation
       nor do I want to sound like him
     berating himself and his radical parents

for once having lived a vision
       but did he perhaps have a point
     about the left's too willing

suspension of judgment? I suppose
       those of us who felt betrayed
     by the high-minded continuities

of what we still called *civilization*
       which had led us into Vietnam
     became fascinated by *the unlike*

the black rebels who appealed
       for the same reason as Cavafy's barbarians
     they offered a *solution*   *Cavafy 18*

I remember a meal with Huey Newton
       at a too expensive restaurant
     just four of us counting the enormous

quite affable bodyguard
       and Don Freed (against whom
     at that very moment

the FBI was circulating
       a murderous COINTELPRO leaflet   *Counterintelligence Program*
     "*Freed is an FBI PIG*")   *Freed xv–xvii*

these were times for new explorations
       but was it not bizarre
     asking Huey about the future

of Czechoslovakia?
       Craziness on all sides
     both terror and repression

some of it still coming down
        Peter Matthiessen sued for $24
million by the Governor

of South Dakota   *Los Angeles Times 11/16/90*
        Johnny Spain still in prison
Leonard Peltier and Ruchell Magee

while simple murderers
        are released in a few years
still and all it astonishes me

that never before my stretch
        in a black Baptist soup kitchen
did I listen to Ishmael Reed

with whom I had taught for a decade
        and question the prejudice
that had only listened

to those blacks most unlike ourselves
        for which Fay paid with her body
Oriane gave up drama

to become a weaver
        and Neal having studied
years about the left in China

became an attorney
        for firms doing business in Beijing
Two years after this

on a return visit
        the daughters now speaking an English
as good as their Chinese

Marvin recalling discussions
        whether those lawyers who quit
because of Fay and the bookkeeper

had in effect betrayed the movement
>> or the movement them
>> says as if in apology

My mind's still open on this
>> and I in a rare
>> moment of certitude affirm

Good!
that's just how we should be

III.vi

For Roberta Chaplan, d. September 26, 1995

Bursts of music all night
>> gentle and wild
>> from the wind chime

your wedding gift
>> we put at the outside corner
>> nearest our bed

this random wind
>> no longer inside you
>> now playing sounds to us

till its chaotic measure
>> becomes us
>> Who cares if this discordant

harmony is predictable
>> as cosmologists have speculated
>> the point is you breathe it into us

on a bad night
>> the first winter storm
>> Ronna awake wondering

whether to fly east
            for her uncle's funeral
        (his heart broken

by the death of both his sons)
            I too insomniac with some
        disturbance I cannot name

your books for children
            your national Cancer Hotline
        for other lonely patients

your long hours on the cushion
            did not avail you
        Ronna's year of nursing you

through vomit and fatigue
            after each chemo session
        till she was like a parent

and you even in remission
            a slightly sullen child
        now all for nothing

there is part of me wonders
            did all that meditating
        liberate your soul too much

from the cares of this life
            till you cared more
        about right living

than living at all
            and lapsed chiefly
        into the quiet fellowship

of those with more knowledge of death
            than most of us choose to share
        and besides your shadow

on the life of Paul
	there is also this aesthetics
   of pure randomness

that took you from us
	and gives you back in each fresh
   chord and arpeggio

now sweet and now angry
	insistent or tentative
   in tune to some outside law

now manic as the church bells
	that used to rock Montreal
   in my wintry childhood

now cagily emphasizing
	by dying away
   as part of the music

the presence of silence
	We have begun to measure
   solar winds out there

between the planets
	a bright rage engulfing
   what Newton taught us

to think of as a clockwork
	solar system
   bending our Northern Lights

able some say
	to emerge even
   on our computer screens

or redirect our lives
	had that unseasonable storm
   not dispersed the Armada

England's religion
      might be different today
   and gentle as you were

of even you it must be said
      the lake of your mind
   so passive you could be seen

as a natural victim
      or an arahant   *arahant: Holy one (Theravada Buddhism)*
   was clouded by a breeze

of resentment at chance
      that annihilated your good projects
   and leaves us this haunting

music invented by no mind

III.vii

The unfinished artwork
      of the zodiac emerging
   Scorpio in the autumn west

luminous even in twilight
      on this 4000-foot ridge
   above two redwood canyons

(and deep below us
      though we do not know it yet
   the darkness of the Covelo reservation)

we have come to feed
      these two Thai monks at the Vihara   *monastery*
   (one German one American

from Amaravati in the Chilterns)
  A few hours later
  the faint line of Pisces

a child's sketch
    with dots to be joined
  Aries no more than a head

and Gemini near dawn
    an abstract parallelogram
  that holds the declining moon

Millennia to plot the sun's
    changing course through these houses
  the equinoctial precession

creating priesthoods with secrets
    too complex for me to follow
  Consider (*a term of augury*

meaning "to observe the stars")   *American Heritage Dictionary*
    the stature of men like Thales
  who could predict eclipses

just as calculating Easter
    (*from Greek khalix   pebble*)   *AHD*
  must have once seemed useful

for separating the Orthodox
    from the Catholic Church
  and even if someday

we might question the expense
    of blasting men into space—
  better to have sent them to the moon

than to Vietnam
    I believe in enlightenment
  as opposed to complacency

kingdoms entrusting their fates
        to the advice of astrologers
    are the ones crushed by the guilty

materialistic *technology*
        that in flight from the past
  marches on blindly   *Washington Post 9/19/95*

to be denounced this morning
        in the *Washington Post*
  by the enraged Unabomber

who too is part
        of this intricate *system*
  he wishes *to dispense with*

through a revolution
        much easier than reform
  in the name of *a movement*

that exalts nature
        and opposes technology   *Washington Post 9/19/95*
  the need to escape

being part of this system
        which is why we are here
  for these two monks

coming down through the live oaks
        in robes of saffron
  with their begging bowls

to be filled with our offering
        at this outdoor table
  (though escape is difficult

Ajahn Amaro before he left
        telling how his sister
  from the Foreign Office

translating for Mrs. Yeltsin
      at a Chequers house party   *country residence of U.K. P.M*
   had the British Prime Minister

rummaging in closets
      to find her a bathing suit)
   But if it is natural

to name this sign in the West
      (so clearly a Scorpion to us
   to the Chinese a Hare)

then from this instinct
      for naming and counting
   my first wife mocked as male

some *system* would surely
      recreate not only itself
   but those needing to escape it

Open enlightenment!
      which does not shrink to the dogmas
   of the supposedly known

and is not so sure of itself
      as to persecute difference
   and lead us into war

in the name of human rights
      John Adams: *What infinite pains*
   and expenses have been incurred

to convert these poor ignorant savages
      Alas! how little success!
   as bigoted to their religion

as Mahometans to their Koran
      the Hindoos to their Shaster
   the Chinese to Confucius

the Romans to their saints and angels
or the Jews to Moses and the Prophets   *Adams '56 10.361*
    Believing analysis

need not turn its back on
        our need for wonder
the darkness without and within

I attend like Socrates
        that knowledge as yet unknown
that will supply reasons

for not just the simple
        motions of the planets
but the affairs of humans

as well as contemplate
        (*templum*   *open space*
marked out by augurs

for observation)   *AHD*
        the slow decline and return
of our shadow across the moon

now easily measurable
        or else chantable
πανκρατὲς αἰεὶ   *Cleanthes: forever omnipotent*

φύσεως ἀρχηγέ   *arch-driver of nature*
        νόμου μέτα πάντα κυβερνῶν)   *by law piloting all things;*
as by these monks last night   *Adams '56 10.71-72*

above the white moonlit fog
        at the bottom of the canyon
Adams: *I am weary*

of contemplating nations
        I am weary of philosophers
our knowledge might be comprehended

111

in twelve pages duodecimo
        The priest and king
    of the Punkapaug and Neponset

were frequent visitors at my father's house
        and I in my boyish rambles
    used to call at their wigwam

where I never failed to be treated
        with whortleberries strawberries
    or apples peaches plums   *Adams '56 10.19-20*

Total enlightenment!
        the Great Work
    of revolution

orbital motion
        as opposed to axial rotation   *AHD*
    succumbing neither

like Lenin to the powers
        already lying in the street
    nor like Yeats with *nothing*

but the embittered sun   *Yeats '89 146*
        striving between them
    to become considerate   *sidus, sideris star*

in that House where we began

                III.viii

Sleepless obsessed
        by the low muted sea-cliffs
    of Baffin Island in the ice

pink dawn on one drifted peak
        of snowy Greenland below us
    I am reading Wordsworth's *Prelude*

as we hurl towards the Northumbrian
        weather where once he
    like now myself *enfranchised*

and at large from a house of bondage   *Exodus 13:3.14*
        wrote of *mountings of the mind*—
    I cannot miss my way!   *Prelude 1.6-20; cf. Paradise Lost 12.646*

pedestrian visitant
        his mind hypnotically enlarged
    from a walk of many months

was usurped by a sense of loss
        and then release   *Our destiny*
    is with infinitude   *Prelude 6.529-39*

his imagination *unfathered*
        by the prospect of descent
    that we had crossed the Alps   *Prelude 6.524*

as we shall this evening
        without any awareness
    our so-called vacation   *"instance of vacating"; AHD*

compressed into three weeks
        my mind too spaced
    from high-altitude cognac

and a really awful movie
        to recapture that insight
    when the light of sense goes out

in flashes that by lack   *Prelude 6.534-35*
        we are more than we are
    still dares to assert itself

in his dharma-lineage   *Dhammanvaya: Digha Nikaya 235, 568*
      not just from this wayfaring
   to seek out ruined choirs

with fractured arch   *Prelude 2.112*
      in which we can only offer
    a different worship   *Prelude 6.672*

but from a talent for self-division
      we both wished to *see*
    the man to come parted as by a gulph

from him who had been and in recoil   *Prelude 11.58-60*
      sought to recover the lost hermit's prayer
   the scholar in his penurious cell   *Prelude 3.490*

one great society one tranquil soul   *Prelude 10.968, 3.116*
      you unfathered   I in flight from mine
  at Cambridge or at Oxford come from far

both full of hopes as northern visitors
      remembering how learning once had been
   the message of a springlike liberation   *cf. Prelude 3.475*

the song of the lark in unfettered air
     mon bel pensar no val   *Does not match my beautiful thought;*
   only to be thrown on the awareness   *Bernart de Ventadorn*

we were aliens in that motley spectacle
      of jealousy ambition envy   *Prelude 3.29,533-34*
   Blind Authority beating with his staff

the child that might have led him   *Prelude 3.640-41*
      the mosaic of learning's gracious body
   disassembled tile by tile

we became conscious of the under soul   *Prelude 3.540*
      that is encountered in retreat
   thus both as pilgrims fled to the narrow streets

of small walled Mediterranean villages
>   whose orchard blossom strung on espaliers
> late this evening I shall see again

charging uphill in a rental Citroen
>   where on one April day
> I walked up under fruited orange trees   P.D.Scott '92 44

the pack on my shoulders heavy
>   and yet welcome self-sufficient
> each painful footstep precious

when I was young and desperate   but young
>   still brooding *our nature and our home*
> *is with infinitude and only there*   Prelude 6.538-39

a doomed pregnant alienation which
>   I now am grateful for   the taste
> of that bitter orange pungent in memory

even though as I shall soon discover
>   the orange trees have been cut down
> to widen the tourist road

This education *à rebours* released
>   visionary dreams   that we *should start*
> out of this *worm-like state*   Prelude 10.835-36

I cannot forget that surge of love
>   *Bliss was it in that dawn* indeed   Prelude 10.692
> seeing dead authorities in question

my campus opened up to ghettoed truths
>   the heady promises of Gramsci Mao
> circles in Sproul Plaza chanting *Aum*

dancing on greensod where Dwight Way had been
>   next to our own untimely gesture   flowers
> on the presented bayonets

115

of the baffled National Guard
　　　　the song that is simple *We shall overcome*
　　soon drowned by whirlwind

whole cities burning like Wheeler Hall
　　　　our statesmen in the name of liberty
　　embracing tyrants whose rebel foe

soon exceeded them in slaughter
　　　　thinking of such recent massacres
　　it was you who wrote *the tide returns again*

the wind wheels round and treads in his own steps
　　　　the earthquake is not satisfied at once　　　　　　*Prelude 10.70-74*
　　blaming it not on false philosophy

but on *a reservoir of guilt*
　　　　and ignorance filled up from age to age
　　that burst in deluge through the land　　　　　　*Prelude 10.435-39*

distraught by striving appetites for vengeance
　　　　and also peace *I would not strike a flower*
　　as many a man his horse　　　　　　*Prelude, p. 493*

you fell a victim to the general curse
　　　　of willed Enlightenment abstracted
　　out of feelings' discipline the flood　　　　　　*cf. Prelude 10.807–08*

of fancies which afflict us more and more
　　　　making our forests vanish
　　enslaving victim nations like Tibet

whole cities brought to standstill in their traffic
　　　　And yet this breakdown saved you, falling
　　no lower than I fell　　　　　　*Prelude 3.506*

returning you to *poets*
　　　　each with each connected　　　　　　*Prelude 12.301–02*
　　and your dedication

to our *redemption surely yet to come*   *Prelude 13.441*
    teaching what all poets everywhere
  in whatever suffering and madness

have learned: *what we have loved remains*
    the rest is dross   *Prelude 13.444; Pound Cantos 81/520–21*
  One can ask to what public end

was England strengthened by your canonization
    or Cambridge by your worship?
  yet your perplexity from your dejection

threw you back again and still again
    into this invisible world within us
  you by yourself *entirely lost*

until startled by an acorn dropping   *Prelude 1.90-94, 6.539*
    a power like one of Nature's   *Prelude 12.312*
  I in my manic insomnia

through the throb of these great engines
    counting my arctic breath
  as on a mountain peak   *Digha Nikaya 214*

with a glimpse of the Faeroes
    the oneness of all dharmas
  the survival of this magnetic energy

with which the solitude of young despair
    compelled me into my unique path
  that became yours

and thus the the path of all
    connected in a scheme of truth
  who have known *an influx*

from the depth of untaught things   *Prelude 12.302–10*
    as we slowly sink
  into this *sea of mist*   *Prelude 13.43*

and catch in the clouds below
        the ghost shadow of the beleaguered plane
    coming inexorably closer up

the shape of language
that is ourselves

III.ix

Ronna the Renaissance is different
        with you beside me   The frescoes
   of Piero della Francesca in Arezzo

called *purely spiritual* by our guide and elsewhere   *Cadogan 415*
      a masterpiece that has retained
     a sense of tenderness   *Michelin 55*

celebrate Saint Helena's miracle
      The Torture of the Jew
   a discomfort to me like that

of reading in this week's Parashah   *weekly Torah portion*
        how Moses commanded the Jews
   fighting the cities of Canaan

Thou shalt save alive
      nothing that breatheth
     but thou shalt utterly destroy them   *Deut. 20:16–17*

no longer for me
      a foreign or historic command
   now that most nights I say the *Shema*   *Deut. 6:4*

before the Lord's Prayer
      pondering the unity that is God
   I must deal with the nervous

rabbinical gloss: *the interests*
of man's moral progress
occasionally demand the employment

of stern and relentless methods   *Humash 833*
How did the sufferings on the cross
or in Egypt and the desert

become so quickly
a case for inflicting pain?
Even Saint Francis who received

the instruction *Rebuild my church*   *Joergensen 106*
and prayed *Lord make me*
an instrument of thy peace

who wrote that *courtesy*
quencheth hate and keepeth love alive   *Bury 729*
who journeyed into Egypt

and won the goodwill of the Sultan   *Lazaro 19; Robson 238*
just as a few years later   *1245, 1253 C.E*
two Franciscan friars

visited the Great Khan at Karakorum   *Lazaro 141–42*
and their successor John of Monte Corvino   *d. 1328 C.E*
became Archbishop of Beijing   *Lazaro 142*

even Saint Francis who refused
to depart from *the way*
of humility and simplicity   *Bury 731*

lived to see compromises
which led to his *moral suffering*   *Lazaro 21–26*
while his order became more rich

organized and contentious
after the general decree
for his early Lives *to be destroyed*   *Lazaro 44; Bury 732–36; Robson 276*

and those Spirituals who appealed
        to *the writings and example of Saint Francis*   *Lazaro 56*
    were imprisoned and burned alive   *Lazaro 38, 56*

no sign now
        of that holy simplicity
    everything dominated

by a mania for politics   *Lazaro 376*
        in the general drift
    towards spiritual entropy

those like Saint Francis
        who emerge as clear lights
    (*pondus amoris*   *the weight of love*

weighing us upwards
        against the weight of sin)
    must endure the fact

that their creativity
        goes beyond what was intended
    beyond even the serendipitous

like *the introduction*
        of printing to Tibet   *Lazaro 323*
    I think of our own experience

having seen the anti-war movement
        become itself a kind of war
    It was the same with Gandhi

whose message to expel the British
        created a new national army
    as with Saint Francis and art

Giotto Piero della Francesca
        the poet Jacopone da Todi
    blaming contact with the universities

for *the harsh persecutions of the Spirituals* *Lazaro 150*
    who preached a Third Age of the Spirit
  from Joachim of Flora

The Father laid on Law
    for that is fear
  the Son discipline

for that is wisdom
    the Spirit unfolds liberty
  for that is love *Joachim f 180v; Lazaro 52*

the Brethren of the Free Spirit
    teaching we should *be guided*
  solely by the inner light *Bury 710*

Meister Eckhardt: in the eyes
    of the deity
  sin and virtue are alike *Bury 711*

we see the same tensions in Islam
    between *ulama* and Sufis *Islamic law scholars*
  in their intoxication

Alas! This shari'ah is the religion of the blind *Islamic law*
    Our religion is unbelief and the religion of the Christians
  Unbelief and belief are the same in our path *Friedmann 23*

Jakob Frank *not any law*
    because that is the side of death
  we are going to life *Scholem 294*

in the poems of William Blake *Godwin 131–35*
    and the Adamic communes of Berkeley
  that would erase the sins of the world

in nakedness and acid
    Tikkun ha-olam *to transform the world*
  the need to heal creation

is a timeless process
    pondus amoris
    what saves us in ourselves

enlightenment from within
    to heal what has been done
    by enlightenment from without

assisted by language
    the means by which memory
    forgetting the sins of the past

remembers the best
    Saint Francis: renew the church   *d. 1226 C.E.*
    or (in the words of his

contemporary Zhu Xi)   *d. 1200 C.E.*
    renovate the people
    by first cleansing our hearts   *Daxue i; Legge 356–58; Chan 86n*

this week's mysterious Haftorah   *weekly Prophet portion*
    invoking the Kabbalah
    vision of our great

participatory creation
    (that the world would last
    for six millennia

and be destroyed in the seventh)   *Sanhedrin 97a; Scholem 120*
    a new epoch
    with the breakup of the heathen kingdoms   *Humash 836*

tikkun ha-olam
    (We are now in the sixth epoch)   *Augustine City of God 22.30*
    not so much amend

as convert the world
    My words in thy mouth
    that I may plant the heavens

and lay the foundations of the earth   *Is. 51:16*

III.x

When Joyce's sister and her kids
        surfaced again in our world
    and resumed their real names

after the deal with Justice
        that she would not go to prison
    for the Weatherman TNT plot

it was an American reconciliation
        like Bernadine Dohrn now planning
    an ABA annual event   *American Bar Association; Wall Street Journal 6/18/90*

instead of what I remember
        her effort vainly to divert
    our garlanded anti-war march

into a doomed confrontation
        with the nervous bayonets
    of the stiff white-faced National Guard

tension between both sides with guns
        and the rest of us
    We are growing more and more warlike   *Mayer 479*

preached William Lloyd Garrison
        (advocate of nonviolence
    before the term was even invented)

against the secret plot
        among some of his closest friends
    to raise arms for John Brown   *Mayer 479*

Brown's failed insurrection
        set the United States
    on the trajectory

of dissolution war
        and social revolution   Mayer 494
    but it was Garrison

faced with a two-party system
        silenced by their own gag rule
        from ever talking about slavery   *Mayer 217*

who by sheer power of words
        despite the so-called
    realistic expectations

of economic determinists
        made the country so aware
    of the slavery question

that by the 1860s
        there were two Americas
    as there have been ever since

Take the Sand Creek massacre
        (or as the double-minded
    plaque still reads *Sand Creek*

'Battle' or 'Massacre')   *Hoig vii*
        where men used their knives
    ripped open women

clubbed little children
        knocked them in the head with their guns   *Churchill 234, cf. 186*
    Captain Chivington the author

was rebuked by the Congress   *Hoig 167*
        but a hero in Colorado   *Hoig 168–72*
    defended by a military historian

as late as 1985   *Dunn*
        while Generals Sherman and Sheridan
    and disciples like Young and Smith

extended these tactics
    from Oklahoma to the Philippines   *Churchill 236–40;*
    Our soldiers have taken prisoner   *Miller 94-95, 162*

people who peacefully surrendered
    and without an atom of evidence
    stood them on a bridge

and shot them one by one
    to drop into the water below
    and float down as an example

to those who found their corpses
    wrote an approving journalist
    It is not civilized warfare

but we are not dealing
    with a civilized people)   *Philadelphia Ledger 11/19/1900; Miller 211*
    General Bell's campaign

once again forcefully
    condemned in Congress   *Miller 213–14*
    but remembered during Vietnam   *1973*

by another military historian
    as *pacification*
    in its most perfected form   *Gates 288*

which *greatly resembled*
    the campaign in the Philippines
    following World War II   *Gates 288*

when *The special tactic*
    was to cordon off areas
    anyone caught inside

was considered an enemy
    almost daily you could find bodies
    floating in the river   *Kerkvliet 196; McClintock 121*

and then the great *psywar* campaign
      using the rivers of Java   *P.D.Scott '89 25, 109*
    The smell was unbelievable

to make sure they didn't sink
    the carcasses were deliberately
    impaled on bamboo stakes   *Pipit Rochijat 43–44*

described delicately
    in *The New York Times*
A GLEAM OF LIGHT IN ASIA: *NYT 6/19/66*

a great deal more contact
    between the anti-Communist
    forces in that country

and at least one very high
    official in Washington
    before and during the massacre

than is generally realized   *NYT 6/19/66*
    Now again as in '65   *in May 1998*
    the Indonesian Red Berets   *Special Forces: RPKAD('65) KOPASSUS('98)*

have instigated mob killings
    and rapes of Chinese women   *Sydney Morning Herald 11/4/98*
    the force funded by the Pentagon

through at least March '98
    despite four years of an explicit
    Congressional prohibition   *NYT 3/17/98*

just as it was in '65
    to *gain influence with successive*
  generations of Indonesia officers   *NYT 3/17/98; cf. P.D.Scott '85 248n, 253*

This is another test
    for that second America
  the remnant of spirit

from the mystical Quakerism
        of Elias Hicks   *Mayer 223*
    uncle of Edward Hicks

The Peaceable Kingdom
        which inspired Garrison
    (so unpopular at first

that even in Boston he was jailed
        to preserve him from a mob
    intent on hanging him)   *Mayer 204–07*

to go back to the Declaration   *of Independence*
        and set the *parchment lies*
    of the Constitution on fire   *Mayer 445*

rousing the abolitionist cause
        which in the end despite
    the opposition of both parties

converted the nation
        by sheer power of words
    making it possible for Lincoln

to dismiss General McClellan   *Mayer 543*
        end the threat of a *military cabal*   *Mayer 540*
    and secure the Thirteenth Amendment   *abolishing slavery; Mayer 575*

before his long-plotted
        removal could prevent it   *Tidwell 272, 332, 480*
    the spirit however weak

of that remnant of reformers
        like Garrison unable to prevent
    the massacres of the Plains Indians

or achieve universal suffrage
        and *political equality for women*
    once more a voice in the wilderness   *Mayer 614, 616*

127

they at least mitigated
    the forced displacement
of the Ponca tribe
Mardock 168–91

and later meeting yet again
    a group of perennial losers
created enough awareness
Miller 111

of atrocities in the Philippines
    to force the retirement
of General *Howling Wilderness* Smith

I want all persons killed
    (ten years and older)
who are capable of bearing arms
Miller 220; Karnow 191

and make the first case
    for Philippine independence
never a popular issue
Miller 262-63

the spirit of A.J. Muste
    Martin Luther King
the three who were killed

for registering voters
    in the Mississippi back country
and Father Roy Bourgeois

who forced Congress to investigate
    the School of the Assassins
their compassionate nonviolence
Washington Post 11/29/98

again like Garrison renews
    the vision of Isaiah
Every valley shall be exalted
Is. 40:4; Mayer 631

inspiring a cause the Weathermen
    (invoking Osawatomie)
were unable to destroy
John Brown; Weather periodical;
Collier and Horowitz 113

a cause threatened today
　　　　by the latest murders
　　　　attributed to KOPASSUS   *London Sunday Times 10/25/98*

of moderate NU clerics   *Nahdlatul Ulama; Indonesian Muslim organization*
　　　　who had defended non-Muslims
　　　　this fate still undecided

between the two Indonesias
　　　　one murderous one tolerant
　　　　(where we see a mirror

of the two Americas)
being also our own

III.xi

That night in Gibeah
　　　　when the hospitable door
　　　　exposed a matron

to avoid worse rape   *Paradise Lost 1.503–05*
　　　　Worse rape? I would ask the class
　　　　no one ever knew the story

the traveling Levite
　　　　and his concubine
　　　　who *when the sun went down*

turned aside to Gibeah
　　　　no one took them in
　　　　but an *old man from the hill country*

who found them *in the open square*
　　　　brought them into his house
　　　　and *said to the men of the city*   *Judges 19:14–16,21–24*

129

pounding on the door
        to have intercourse with the wayfarer
      Here are my virgin daughter and his concubine

let me bring them out now
      Ravish them and do what you want with them
      but against this man

do not such a vile thing   *Judges 19:22–24*
      It is hardly surprising
    that Rachel Adler of *Tikkun*

interviewed in the *Jewish Bulletin*
      of Northern California
    has *a problem* with this story

as well as its male commentators
      from Rashi to the present   *Adler 1A*
    (for example that gloss of Milton

to avoid worse rape)   *Paradise Lost 1.505*
      for the story is not finished
    The man seized his concubine

and put her out to them
      through the night they raped her
    and as dawn began to break

they let her go
      the woman came and fell down
    at the door of the man's house   *Judges 19:25–26*

and when *her master got up*
      there was his concubine
    with her hands on the threshold

Get up, he said to her
      but there was no answer
    Then he put her on the donkey

and set out for his home
        When he entered his house
    he took a knife   *Judges 19:27–29*

("How could this have been written?")   *Adler 1A*
        and grasping his concubine
    he cut her into twelve pieces

limb from limb
        (the RSV assumes   *Revised Standard Version*
    that the woman had died by then

though this is far from clear)
        and sent her throughout the territory of Israel   *Judges 19:29*
    As Rachel Adler puts it

the Bible was written by men
        the violent images
    raise serious questions

about the moral implications
        of treating women as objects   *Adler 1A*
    Jephthah's daughter sacrificed

as a burnt offering   *Judges 11:31*
        Milton even approved
    (though circumspectly) the laws

of the Torah on women
        found not to be virgin
    if these things are true

&c &c   *Milton 783; Deut. 22:20. 14*
        (suppressing what follows:
    then they shall bring her out

to the door of her father's house
        and the men of her city
    shall stone her with stones

that she die
        as happens to this day
    in Saudi Arabia and Bangla Desh

whereas the man who lies with a virgin
        shall give fifty shekels of silver
    to the young woman's father)

The fate of the concubine
        was discussed in assembly
    by the armed men of Israel

they told the Benjaminites
        to *hand over those scoundrels*
    But the Benjaminites would not listen

so they *offered burnt offerings before the Lord*
        arrayed troops against Gibeah
    and *put the whole city to the sword*

the city the people the animals
        and then *with compassion*
    for Benjamin their kin

What shall we do for wives
        for those who are left?
    rounded up the virgins

of Jabesh-Gilead
        and the young women of Shiloh
    who came out to dance

closing out not just the age
        but the Book of Judges
    In those days there was no king

people did what was right in their eyes
        (just as kingship in turn
    led to Jeremiah's wrath

Deut. 22:20-21

Deut. 22:29

Judges 20:13

Judges 20:26

Judges 20:37

Judges 20:48

Judges 21:6–7

Judges 21:12

Judges 21:21

Judges 21:25

and the destruction of the temple)
      The Jewish story
    differs from other peoples'

(like the *brilliant brilliance*   *ming ming*
      of King Wen and King Wu
    in the Chinese *Book of Odes*)   *3.1.2.1*

it is more honest
      the *peshat* is dreadful   *literal sense*
    which is why all of us

are driven to wonder about it
      and to this cultural dilemma
    There is indeed a *problem*

with the tale of the concubine
      and yet it is not enough
    to complain the obvious

that it is *problematic*   *Adler 1A*
      How to deal with our troubled past
  so difficult to confront

(in the words of the woman rabbi
      Can we bring races together
  if we remember all that has been done?)

and difficult to ignore?
      Scandal proliferates
    when suppressed by decorum

and there is no lasting peace
      in the security
    that comes from naive denial

My Aunt Anna told me
      of the Belgians she had just met
    who were let out of the Congo

by the border police
        on condition they left behind
    their fourteen-year-old daughter

and I a twenty-two-year-old
        fresh out of Canada
    not getting it asked her why

I think now of the complacent
        Paulinus of Pella
    identified only

as a grandson of Ausonius
        heedful to keep unstained
    my cherished reputation

I had no sex
except with my household slaves   Paulinus of Pella 164–66

III.xii

Once again! Insight
        beckons down the long corridors
    of my insomnia

as to why I have been depressed
        since flying back from Europe
    the sense of impotence

not just from losing my glasses
        or even a week ago
    tripping over a sprinkler head

to fall flat on the pavement
        and fracture my zygomatic arch
    not even Noam's crack

about those who do *microanalysis*
        about things that don't matter   Chomsky '94 163
    No! I have learned from my inability

last night to explain to Fred   Frederick Crews
        what the unstoppable flow of drugs
    across the Mexican border

has to do with the Kennedy assassination
        a world where what matters
    are not just the structural patterns

but the patterns in chaos
        such as the DFS lies   Dirección Federal de Seguridad, Mexican Secret Police
    about Oswald and Silvia Durán   P.D.Scott '95 118–27

forwarded by Echeverría   Luís Echeverría; Minister of Interior
        the CIA's asset
    LITEMPO-2 in the censored CIA cable   MEXI 7029; P.D.Scott '96 40

who after the student massacre
        at the time of the '68 Olympics
    Not until an hour later

did the Army stop firing   Agee 557
        became President of Mexico
    his brother-in-law Zuno Arce

the top drug connection
        before jailed by a Los Angeles judge
    for the murder of Camarena   P.D.Scott '96 41; Los Angeles Times 3/25/93

the same relationship
        as in this decade
    President Salinas' brother Raúl

now under arrest in the U.S.
        for having ordered
    the Ruiz Massieu assassination   P.D.Scott '96 41; Wall Street Journal 2/8/96

Citibank the nation's largest
    now under investigation
    for having laundered Raúl's funds   *New York Times 3/30/96*

the bank with the largest
    debt exposure in Mexico
back when the CIA reported

The profits of drug exports
    for just two countries alone
Mexico and Colombia

probably amount to
    75 percent
of their foreign export earnings   *Mills 1135*

As noted in a DEA report
    from Harrison its Mexico informant   *Lawrence Victor Harrison*
and prosecution witness

at Zuno Arce's trial   *Scott and Marshall 41, 204*
    the journalist Buendía   *Manuel Buendía*
reported that some Contras

were being trained near Veracruz
    by the CIA using
    the DFS as a cover   *DEA Report of 3/2/90; P.D.Scott '96 40*

at a ranch owned by the traffickers
    after which he was promptly murdered
    for which the head of the DFS   *José Antonio Zorrilla Pérez*

was eventually arrested   *P.D.Scott '96 41; NYT 6/15/89*
    As I said to Betty   *Betty Crews*
over her chilled beet soup

the gladness of a buttery   *Hölderlin '52 153*
    not too assertive Chardonnay
what has so undone me

is not my inability
            to change all this
       but my speaking with two voices

which cannot be compassed
            having to be split-minded
       in the struggle to keep communication

between the present
            and the best of the past
       there is not much progress

if the left leg hankers for the beach
            and the right for Sacramento
       the problem has always been

how do we live with evil
            we can profit from it
       we can preach against it

but if we write poetry
            how not to misrepresent
       the great conspiracy

of organized denial
            we call civilization?
       From the protected mob

around JFK airport
            with ties to the Russian
       mafia at Brighton Beach

and the plane which every day
            flies a million dollars in cash
       to the drug banks of Russia

at a time when Russia
            owes $17 billion a year
       in interest to its creditors

to the universities
        continuously inventing new ways
    not to contemplate such things

all language depends
        on sustainable split-mindedness
    like the ex-Green Beret in Palo Alto   *U.S. Special Forces*

who would no longer
        as agreed the night before
    speak to Al McCoy and myself

about heroin in Vietnam
        instead taking us outside
    to look at his red M.G.

parked on a calm Palo Alto street
        with a fresh hole inches wide
    burned through its thick steel door

an implosion device! his old unit?
        impenetrable mysteries
    unforgettable at the time

and then in the interests of survival
        swiftly forgotten
    as I shall not forget

the haunting performance
        of the St. Matthew Passion
    I shall be taken to tonight

by my wife Ronna
        the circle of crème fraîche
    in Betty's beet-deep soup

like Zen calligraphy
        but you could lay prize-winning volumes
    of poetry from here to Walnut Creek

and in how many of them
            could you find the seminal words
        DFS or *debt exposure*

or even *CIA?*

SECOND RETREAT:
KNIFE-SHARPENING AT VAJRAPANI

DAY ONE

Like the trees
with their gesticulations

the jay with his chatter
cannot communicate

except by becoming silent
the times he comes up close

hoping to share breakfast

DAY ONE: STONE

to clean this stone
drop it in a pot

of boiling water
over the next hour

the grease and dirt
will slowly breathe out

into the water
leaving underneath

on the aluminum
a photographic image

of its identifying
pocks and scratches

DAY TWO

Stillness eludes me
the dark leaves

of the tall bay tree
reflected in my mug

trembling
each time the yogi

at the other end of the table
stirs his tea

DAY THREE

Light between the shoulders
of those sitting in front

remains on my retina
a blue goblet

which when focused upon
becomes a lake

with rushes round it
the ripples enlarging

till the far shore disappears
and you can see within

which is to say
darkness

My first meditation
before my father

taught me to walk
Indian-style

one foot in front of the other
along the narrow path

silently
hoping to raise a heron

my mother
held me by the hand

as we stood on the cedar log
to look down at the dancing

reflected sunlight
the chrome yellow

water lilies

DAY THREE: STEEL

*The gap between knife and steel
should be small*

*if you hone in
at too wide an angle*

*the blade will be sharp at first
then quickly dull*

DAY FOUR

Beneath the eyes
of the White Tara and Green Tara

Shakyamuni and Medicine Buddha
black angry Mahakol

on this cushion
I am three-and-a-half feet high

and when a grown-up
steps on my foot

the powerlessness I feel from age
with such a small legacy

142

to leave to my children
so little done those absent years

so little to show
(this going inside

the pain of self-revelation
will it leave me impotent?)

is suddenly overwhelmed
by the hot tearful

powerlessness of childhood
Am I sixty-seven or four?

I am suddenly angry
at this teacher who cannot ease

the confusion of injustice in the world

DAY FOUR: BLOOD

testing the honed blade
a thin line of blood

near the childhood scar
where I closed the penknife

on my second finger
what my mother had exactly

warned me not to do

when the rich boys on Cape Ann
broke the expensive

uninhabited window
into dangerous swords of glass

they blamed the Canadian
visiting for a weekend

my mother asked me about it
I answered weakly, *I was there*

that was enough   we paid
From that terrible day

something priceless
even if unachievable

my mother's words *Learn
to think for yourself*

DAY FIVE

I walk on the gravel road
taking baby Indian steps

I am twenty miles high
and risk toppling over

I am walking on the moon
my head so far from earth

it might roll off course
and not come back

DAY FIVE: CHEF'S KNIVES

The chef's knives in this drawer
this gompa near Boulder Creek   *meditation hall*

where we are given the freedom
to be silent

none of this would be here
if not for the persecution in Tibet

the anonymous benefactors
who brought the lamas here

and now the logging
blue ominous crosses

on the redwoods around us

DAY SIX

I say to my teacher
Is it common for you to hear this?

my retreat has been so profound
I have come wonderfully into touch

with how completely rotten
I feel about my life?

And he answers
Things are as they are

but you can feel regret
and I feel regret

turn into compassion

DAY SIX: CLEAVER

This heaviest cleaver
my steel cannot sharpen

could it be meant to stay blunt?
Consider: how much pain

in a family
even where there is love

DAY SEVEN

The room so desperately hot
you can hear the sweat

slide down your face
even the teacher is losing it

his head almost hitting the floor
from lack of oxygen

and when trucks finally arrive
to empty the Porta-Potties

the scent of shit wafts over us
(like the shit in the shadow mind

which when meditation brings us
deeper into the present

we have to breathe)
I find myself saying

in response to the trucks' uproar
I am being mindful

of the noise and odor
of human feces

being sucked up through a hose
and a breakthrough

from laughter
the human condition

stercus mundi   *the shit of everyday life*

suddenly so comic

it is a release

DAY SEVEN: ORANGE

Perspiring beneath
the Tibetan prayer flags

and bunches of home-grown herbs
I remember my sons Mika and John

singing to me
(where is that tape

I promised to listen to again?)
as I slice an orange

the blade falls cleanly through

146

DAY EIGHT

As the end comes into sight
each breath becomes more precious

each footstep I take
moves me closer

at any minute
I might sob disappointed

that we will soon have
to talk again

or else with joy
admiring the courage

it took my young wife Ronna
to marry an older man

DAY EIGHT: TECHNIQUES

Here I am still sharpening
as my father did

at the head of the Christmas table
back and forth

flashing blade and steel
outwards towards the guests

even after Shanti
the cook has showed me

her trick of sliding
the edge quietly

inwards
towards the navel

DAY NINE

On this last morning
as one or two car

engines start up
beyond my tinnitus

may I continue
to breathe in and out

with the same concentration
walk this strict

tight-rope
between light and darkness

death and life

IV

二儀

ER YI—THE WAYS OF HEAVEN AND EARTH

"There is never a case when the root is in disorder and yet the branches are in order." —Confucius, *Daxue* vii

"For want of correspondence with the first principles which belong to the imagination . . . the rich have become richer, the poor have become poorer . . . such are the effects which must ever flow from an unmitigated exercise of the calculating faculty." —Shelley 1887 30–31; Yeats '68 68

"Die Dichter mussen auch / Die geistigen weltlich seyn" ("The poets too, spiritual / Must be of the world") —Hölderlin '84 86

"Was bleibet aber, stiften die Dichter" ("What endures, the poets establish") —Hölderlin '84 108; Heidegger '49 280; Rorty 140

IV.i

And now for something a bit more serious *Virgil Ecl. 4.1*
     a poem that looks at
   the eye in the triangle

above the blunted pyramid

   (it is not just blasphemous

but illegal to reproduce
     too much of this icon
   it would weaken our current faith

which is to say our credit) *Greider '87 53*
     and its temple the Federal Reserve
   born out of the Gilded Age

the ultimate age
      of the song of Cumae   *Virgil Ecl. 4.4*
   (*gild: Archaic*

to smear with blood)   *AHD*
     a temple so inscrutable
     Zinn barely mentions it

among the Progressive reforms
    aimed at quieting
   the popular risings   *Zinn '80 341*

while the far Right are confounded
     by their fears of the New World Order   *Mullins 8-13;*
    exotic Masonic lodges   *Kolko '63 184; Greider '87 276*

the Illuminati and the Jews   *Mullins 42–68; Greider '87 52*
      Though we continue to prate
    about the Open Society

54 percent of the total
     net financial assets
    are *held by the 2 percent*   *Federal Reserve Board; Greider '87 39; cf. Phillips 11*

whose two top institutions
     the Fed and the CIA   *Federal Reserve Board*
    the most powerful and unpopular

lie beyond the reach
     and even the comprehension
    not just of the people

but Congress the legal system and the press
     In the crisis of '82
    when Mexico almost defaulted

on its $80 billion debt
     the largest banks would have been
    swamped in the resulting panic   *Greider '87 517*

152

had they not been saved
        by actions taken in secret
        Between the Fed and the Treasury

an unprecedented bailout was arranged
        $3.5 billion
        in new loans for Mexico

So why did the NIC   *National Intelligence Council*
        concerned about *foreign exchange*   *Mills 1129*
produce a CIA evaluation

the profits of drug export revenues
        of Colombia and Mexico
        probably represent

75 percent
        of source-country export earnings?   *NIC Report; Mills 1181, cf. 1135*
        Nazar Haro the DFS Chief   *Mexican Dirección Federal de Seguridad*

who sold protection to the traffickers
        and obstructed the HSCA investigation   *House Select*
        protected in turn by the CIA   *Committee on Assassinations*

from an indictment in San Diego
        for his *indispensability*
        as a source of intelligence

the objecting U.S. Attorney
        fired for revealing this   *Scott '95 135; Scott and Marshall 36*
        And why did the Treasury in '84

introduce bearer bonds
        despite the expert advice
        they would become instruments

used by the traffickers
        for money-laundering?   *Naylor 284*
        The Fed and the CIA

both so powerful
> we know almost nothing about them   *Greider '87 11–12*
> not to mention the IMF   *International Monetary Fund*

whose draconian remedies
> for impoverished countries
> like Yugoslavia and Rwanda

and perhaps now Indonesia   *Wall St. Journal 5/7/98: Toronto Star 5/17/98*
> have been followed by massacres   *Chossudovsky 111–20. 243-60*
> *If the secrets were revealed*

the money mystery would dissolve
> *people would have to look upon*
> *these things directly*   *Greider '87 717*

Why put all this in a poem?
> There are times when the most novel
> act of creativity

is to aim at the simplest truth
> *the rich are getting richer*
> *the poor poorer*

and if not checked this will destroy us
> Why does this happen? *Bassesse oblige!*
> And the cure? we must live by

what we have always known:
> *No crime worse than avarice*   *Tao Te Ching 46*
> likewise *the political hegemony*

of money must end   *Greider '87 715*
> One need not even abolish the Fed
> only find *the will*

to abandon money's value
> *to save the real economy*   *Greider '87 716*
> the problem is not even capital

the new *fluidity* from America
                 which as Marx observed
          erased those feudal

English *preconceptions*
                 when *it was 'respectable'*
          to sell Negroes into slavery

(the crest of Sir John Hawkins
          a demi-naked man
          the hands extended and manacled)   *Fairburn 1, 165*

but not to make sausages boots or bread   *Marx '76 1014; MacGregor '84 216*
                 No! the problem is the abuse
          of capital power   *Pramoedya '99 253*

always consolidating privilege
                 by taxing the misery of the poor   *cf. MacGregor '84 8, 169*
          When a president of a bank

can reward himself after slashing
          12,600 jobs
          with a one-year salary and bonus

of seventy-six million dollars   *Los Angeles Times 3/25/00*
                 how shall we talk of America's
          doctrine of equality?   *Beard 250–52*

We have not failed at production
                 we have failed at distribution
          if we have learnt anything

in the 2000 years since Virgil
                 it is to expect no moral progress
          from our political leaders

or *the banks British merchants*
                 and *insurance companies*   *Madison to Jefferson 5/1/1796;*
          feared by our Founding Fathers   *Ellis 162*

and none either from *that*
> *supreme abstraction money*   MacGregor '84 167
which empowers a worker to act

as a free agent   Marx '76 1033; MacGregor '84 211
> *in the surface process*
> *of equality and freedom*

beneath which in the depths
> *entirely different processes go on*
where *equality and liberty disappear*   Marx '73 247–50; MacGregor
                                                        '84 159–60

Money as an abstraction   Hegel '42 240; MacGregor '84 167
unifying our world
at the same time making *obsolete*   AHD

the first meaning of *commonwealth*   *the public welfare*
> Thus in the last fifty years
> *for want of correspondence*

with the imagination   Shelley 1887 30–31; Yeats '68 68
> the CIA has helped install
> the thugs of drug cartels

in Thailand Bolivia Afghanistan
> Haiti and Peru
accelerating the flow

of profits from the poorest
> nations to the richest
(why houses cost so much:

In 1984 alone
> *the Commerce Department calculated*
> *a net influx of foreign capital*

into the US
> *at about $100 billion)*   Naylor 332
while with draconian drug laws

in the name of order
      we had a million people in prisons
    by the year 1994   *Washington Post 10/28/94*

1.8 million
      just four and a half years later   *Washington Post 3/15/99*
    And should my poem take refuge

in rich sensuous detail
      or shall I say more clearly
  what we removed from our book?

that when Clinton and the Fed
      lent Mexico $40 billion   *New York Times 1/17/95*
    it should have been clear even then

how this debt would be repaid
      Mexico's Attorney General's
    office states that drug traffickers

earned $28 billion
      in 1992 and 1993
    amounts similar to all

of the country's legal exports combined   *Latinamerica Press 9/2/95*
      for the benefit of this corrupt
    ordo seclorum   *Virgil Ecl. 4.5*

all of us without thinking
carry round in our billfolds

IV.ii

Looking north from my nightwatch
      on the jostling flume
    of the Quebec North Shore Paper Company

up the long empty valley
        of the Manicouagan
    towards the northern lights

dancing and singing to me
        (*human life is short*
        imagine anything)

it seemed that the low light
        of Baie Comeau to the south
    was the dim gleam of history

I would be coming back to
        when I returned to Montreal
    And indeed the books

which we read the next autumn
        The Eighteenth Century Background   *Willey*
    or *The Heavenly City*

of the Eighteenth Century Philosophers   *Becker*
        sustained that illusion
    of looking at history

from a point outside it
        as Crane Brinton put it
    in *The Anatomy of Revolution*

attempting to establish
        as the scientist might
    certain first approximations   *Brinton 7*

(that's how we all felt in those heady
        days after the war
    in a realm of freedom

having been taught we had arrived
        at a promising exceptionalist
    moment *The End of Ideology*)

158

though indeed the too frequent
      pairing of the words
    Jacobins and *Bolsheviks*   Brinton 155, 183; cf. 105, 123, 137, 149, 181, etc.

revealed an authorial nervousness
      we were not so outside history
  as to be secure from it

Unfettered by common sense
      only a sincere extremist
  in a revolution

(Robespierre Cromwell
      and even one fears Jefferson)
  can kill men because he loves man

attain peace through violence
      and free men by enslaving them   Brinton 158–60
  Over and over I ingested

that benign condescension
      towards enthusiasts like Jefferson
  though what was projected

on to Bolshevik *extremists*
      was not just the practice
  of the United States

from the extermination of the Seminoles
      in the East Florida war   Sellers 98
  to the *liberation* of the Philippines

and the *pacification* of Vietnam
      but a practice taught
  as an exploitable technique

exemplary criminal violence
      the murder and mutilation of captives
  and the display of their bodies

in Army Pamphlet 525-7-1   *McClintock 209*
          at the School of the Americas
     This complacency of our teachers

now seems undemocratic
          (*Democracy* wrote Whitman
     after reading Hegel

is a great word
          whose history remains unwritten
     because yet to be enacted)   *Whitman 960; Rorty 19*

and indeed culpable
          distancing us students
     not just from Jefferson

but the *heavenly city*
          in our new separation
     of politics from morality

Georgetown University (and my own)
          can provide an academic home
     to a man who describes

the counter-guerrilla campaign
          of the Guatemalan Army
     as *appropriate tactics and methods*   *Luttwak 157–58; McClintock 428*

and a man in an Institute
          on the U Penn campus
     has said of the death squads

of El Salvador
          they did what they *had to do*   *Radu 69*
     it being *untenable* to treat

their victim Archbishop Romero
          as a spiritual leader   *Radu 17*
     while those like Chomsky who rose up

to denounce these new mandarins
        have rebuked Jefferson in their turn
        for supporting violations of human rights   *Chomsky '92 34-35,*
                                                                        361, 399

(as indeed he did
        I am not proposing
        a past that is free from error

only that to compile
        a list of errors alone
        is another distortion of truth)

Meanwhile others more cynical
        construed *the idea of justice*
        itself as *an instrument of power*   *Foucault '74 187; Rabinow 6*

thus preparing for that revolution
        which will happen when the mass
        of ordinary Americans

have learned to disregard
        Jefferson and his ideals
        which is to say never

as if the only hope
        was an anarchic fresh start
        with what Marcuse wanted

a *tabula rasa*   *fresh slate*
        Alas! the human species
        is not a piano

on which one can play
        anything imaginable
        each human community

has its own birdsong
        which can be refined
        or even varied

with something utterly different   Pinsky 85; Heaney '95 191
     but as Heaney quoted
  in the same essay

from Nadezhda Mandelstam
     who had had some experience
  with intellectuals

unrestrained by the past
     the poet does not speak 'for them'
  (the poet's fellow beings)

but with them
     nor do he set himself
  apart from them

otherwise he would not be
     a source of truth   Mandelstam 225–26; Heaney '95 193
  and when Milosz spoke of his surprise

to have seen me on a platform
     against the Vietnam War
  with Noam Chomsky

one of those intellectuals
     who destroyed Weimar   cf. New York Review 5/7/70, 5/21/70
  I thought to myself *no way*

America two hundred years old
     is comparable to Weimar
  but now the sense of something wrong

deepens we are adrift
     in an ocean of non-commitment   Olson 113
  a stripped and empty scene   Murdoch 240

losing sight of the heavenly city
     in *an academic dualism*   MacIntyre 58
  from *the Enlightenment project*

for an objective morality   *MacIntyre 107*
       with critics *who view anomie*
    as an ordo salutis   *Olson 112*

and so-called social scientists
       by whom *political and social action*
    are *presented as mindless*   *MacIntyre 58*

the end product as Hegel predicted
       of the estrangement
    of Enlightenment from religion   *Hegel '77 328; Olson 126*

the sole work of universal freedom
       is therefore death   *Hegel '77 360*
    a Speculative Good Friday   *Olson 124*

when as Hölderlin wrote
       God's failure helps   *Hölderlin '84 22*
    while poetry when it is

strong enough to help   *Seferis 134; Heaney '95 9, 191*
       helps to revive
    our memory of the future

Becker repeated from Herder
       If Marcus Aurelius
    speaks with his own heart

he speaks also to mine   *Herder 14, 251–52; Becker 146*
       To be free we must be grounded
    and not just *spectatorial*   *Rorty 35*

only from tradition
       can there be ruptures
       (answering Kant's

sense of the dignity
       of human life
       with Baudelaire

the diminution of the traces
of original sin)   *Eliot '51 392*
only from memory

can there be hope
so we may be able
to achieve our country

and change the history of the world   *Baldwin 119; Rorty 13*

IV.iii

Covetousness in which we are so immersed
that *no one has the power*
to turn his eyes away!   *Paradiso 27.121-23*

as Dante heard in heaven
after he had last looked down
at *il varco folle d'Ulisse*   *the mad track of Ulysses; Paradiso 27.82-83*

but the repetition of such warnings
No disaster worse than greed   *Tao Te Ching 46*
is now so anachronistic

it proves the extent
to which our left and right
The Nation The National Review

have receded from Jefferson's goal
of *silently lessening*
the inequality of property   *Jefferson 3.268–69; Sellers 36*

thus for a place to stand
when challenging money
let us defend the Populist

164

followers of Jefferson
>against my university colleagues
>and *The New York Times*

and defend John Adams
>and the Constitution
>against my old colleagues on the left

whose jibes at the Fathers
>in their anti-war books
>I never challenged at the time

though I myself quoted Adams   *Schurmann Scott & Zelnik 9*
>about Nations at *height of power*   *Adams '62 4.158*
>but of course I challenged nothing

the student activists commented
>how *faculty* (me) *will sit for hours*
>*through these all-night meetings*

and never offer advice
>so perhaps I should blame myself
>or my negative daimon

for what I now criticize
>though only in poetry
>but accepted then in silence

or was it necessary
>to define by our failure
>in the face of the mindless

self-perpetuating establishment
>the path for our return?
>Like Adams and Jefferson

(one fears the ignorance of the people
>*the other the selfishness of rulers)*   *Jefferson 10:90; Adams-Jefferson 280*
>we must see how Chief Justice Marshall

having overruled Jefferson
      (for judges *to decide*
    what laws are constitutional

would make the judiciary
      a despotic branch)   *Jefferson 10.89; Adams-Jefferson 279*
    in *Marbury v. Madison*   *(1803)*

(*the doctrine that judges have the power*
      to declare an act of Congress
      null and void   *Beard 244*

Jefferson: *The Constitution*
      on this hypothesis
      is a mere thing of wax)   *Beard 244–45*

then turned to the common law
      and was able in Dartmouth   *Dartmouth College v. Woodward (1819)*
    to rule that corporations

because they affect property
      are inviolable by the states   *Sellers 87*
    and in *Sturges v. Crowninshield*   *(1819)*

that a state could not end that quirk
      through which small debtors went to jail
    while through bankruptcy

large debtors were freed from their debts   *Sellers 88*
      and in *McCulloch v. Maryland*   *(1819)*
    that it was *convenient*

to delegate the constitutional
      power to coin money   *Art. 1 Sect. 8 Para. 5*
    to the private Bank of the U.S.   *Sellers 89*

(*this institution is one*
      of the most deadly
      existing against the principles

and form of our Constitution)   *Jefferson 10.57*
        thus freeing corporations
    and judge-made law itself

from the restraints of the past
        as well as the Constitution   *Sellers 44, 50-51*
    so that Jefferson's vision

of *silently lessening*
        the inequality of property   *Jefferson 3.268-69; Sellers 36*
    was lost in the shambles

of the Bank War
        between President Jackson   *Andrew Jackson*
    on behalf of the *real people*

(*planters farmers mechanics*)   *Greider '87 254-55*
        and Biddle's Bank of the United States   *Nicholas Biddle*
    a seminal conflict

that did not go away in time   *Greider '87 255*
        between the powers of the past
    (the bondholders of the northeast)

and of the future
        (the *uninhibited ambition*
    to the South and West)

one of the permanent tensions
        still present beneath the surface   *Greider '87 257; cf. Phillips 185-202*
    In his important book

A People's History
        (for *the 99 percent*
    whose *commonality*

the Founding Fathers
        tried their best to prevent
    sharers of leftovers

167

in a battle for resources
       made scarce by elite control)   *Zinn '80 571*
   Zinn writes of the Indian Removal

(a war which earlier historians
       like Schlesinger and Meyers   *Arthur Schlesinger, Jr.; Marvin Meyers*
   do not mention   *Zinn '80 129; cf. Schlesinger 141, 350; Beard 326*

but which Marshall opposed)   *Kazin 22*
       and Jackson's instructions
   I offer my Choctaw children

land they shall possess as long
       as grass grows or water runs   *Zinn '80 132*
   (an Indian G.I.

testifying publicly in 1970
       repeated that phrase
   and began to weep)   *Zinn '80 133*

but by depicting Jackson
       as *slaveholder speculator*
   exterminator of Indians

Zinn lost sight of the Bank War
       in *much talk of tariffs*
   banking political parties

political rhetoric   *Zinn '80 129*
       along with Jefferson's warnings
   about *an aristocracy*

founded on banking institutions
       and moneyed incorporations   *Sellers 106*
   and Adams' *Every bank of discount*

is downright corruption
       taxing the public
   for private individuals' gain   *Adams '62 9.638*

(which Pound made his slogan   *Cantos 71/416, 74/437, etc.*
    as the problem of issue   *Cantos 87/569*
drew him step by step

into singing perpetual war)   *Cantos 86/568; cf. Williams 180*
        after twenty years at this
    I am beginning to learn

what poetry cannot do
        at least within these limits
    of domination and servitude   *Hölderlin '52 85*

and also what it can
        i.e. sweeten the Renaissance
    of an emerging class

as Dante did in Italy
        Shakespeare and Milton in England
    or remind a nation

of its founding truths
        which have become forgotten
    measure in things is best   *Odyssey 7.310*

the belief of the Founding Fathers
        who used to read Homer
    saw clearly the need to check

the growth of power
        unable to check itself
    when a Nation has grown

to such an height of Power
        as to become dangerous
    she never fails to loose

her Wisdom and Moderation
        and with these her Power   *Adams '62 4.158, Schurmann Scott & Zelnik 9*
    But since the crude enthusiasms

169

of Emerson for *trade*
  and *joint-stock companies*   *Sellers 380*
or of the young Walt Whitman

for the seizure of California
  in a slavery-driven war   *Mayer 358–60*
no one has managed to bring

America's values back together
  After the Vietnam tumult
when Zinn quoted Adams

it was to show Adams' dislike
  of riots and lawlessness
These tarrings and featherings

this breaking open Houses
  in Resentment for private Wrongs
must be discountenanced   *Zinn '80 68*

(some people would still agree)
  Zinn saw the Founding Fathers
as skilful diverters

of *rebellious energy*
  so they *could take over*
land profits and power   *Zinn '80 59*

but in this new era
  of bonanza profits
in the prison industry

should we who by our tactics
  of destructive rage
elected Ronald Reagan

not ask: Did not we ourselves
  help divert this energy
by separating it from the Fathers

of our only Revolution?
      They like us mistrusted wealth
   these green bits of paper

which in '35
      when taken off the Gold Standard
   added instead the words

In God We Trust

IV.iv

Of course the bankers
      had the best of reasons
   to suppress Jefferson's idea

Bottom *the national bills*
      on pledges for their redemption
   no interest on them would be necessary   *Jefferson 15.31; Pound '73 152, 159, 296, 326*

and the Populists' subtreasury plan   *Zinn '80 281*
      a democratic money system
   to use the pure credit inherent

in the national government
      to finance directly
   the productive efforts of citizens   *Greider '87 261*

i.e. *money at cost instead*
      of money lent by bankers   *Greider '87 263*
   at the rates they choose

a plan denounced by the *Times*
      as *one of the most fantastic*
   projects ever proposed   *Goodwyn 271; Greider '87 264*

though not by Keynes and others
      like the founder of the AEA   *American Economic Association*
  or by Greider: *the road not taken*   *Greider '87 264*

For Degler the *real cause*
      of the farmers' discontent
  lay in *overproduction*

(*the population rose 30 per cent*
      the number of farms 51 per cent)
  he mocked the farmers' response

that *thousands were going hungry*   *Degler 360–61*
      even without regard
  to the famines in India and China

Meanwhile the Populist hopes
      were labeled by Hofstadter
  (*without a single reference*

to the thoughtful and attainable
      planks of the People's Party)   *Goodwyn 602, 271*
  as an *agrarian myth*   *Hofstadter '55 46-59; Kazin 190–92*

people who viewed themselves
      as innocent pastoral victims
  of a conspiracy hatched in the distance   *Goodwyn 602; Hofstadter '55 35*

It took Ken Stampp to remind me
      at a neighborhood Book Club dinner
  of Hofstadter's real concern

which Zinn and Goodwyn do not mention
      the anti-Semitic rhetoric
  going back to the Bank War   *Hofstadter '55 77-81; Dinnerstein 21, 49–50*

of the *dispossessed farmers*   *Rorty 52*
      (which constrained Roosevelt
  when asked to save Europe's Jews)   *Dinnerstein 143–46*

against Rothschilds and Warburgs
     which Father Coughlin in the '30s
  mined from the Populist past

how *the Federal Reserve*
     at the behest of the Rothschilds
  could *manipulate the stock market*

and drag the U.S. into war   *Kazin 119*
     rhetoric which Michael Kazin
  in his thoughtful book

dismisses as *quite false*   *Kazin 119*
     though Greider agrees that the Fed
  fathered *the 1929 collapse*

by helping the central banks of Europe
     the great international banking houses
  from Morgan to Rothschild

had always worked closely with one another   *Greider '87 297*
     This is not to defend Coughlin
  whose rhetoric *came increasingly*

from Nazi publications   *Dinnerstein 117*
     so that now criticism of the Fed
  is the purlieu of those anti-Semites

who see Hamilton Morgan Roosevelt
     even Churchill as Jews   *Dinnerstein 129*
  Hence Hofstadter's fear in the '50s

In a populistic culture
     which seems to lack a responsible elite
  it is conceivable that

the rational pursuit
     of our well-being and safety
  would become impossible   *Kazin 190-91; Hofstadter '63 78–79*

173

This Fifties *suspicion*
     of mass democracy
     and populistic culture   Kazin 190, 192

is regretted by Michael Kazin   Kazin 192, 24
     who agrees with Emerson
     March without the people

and you march into the night   Kazin 7
     But how can he understand
     The Populist Persuasion

when he never mentions what Marshall
     did to the constitution
     nor what the banks have done

to merit the Populist attack?
     America is a process
     beyond anyone's description

yet containing within its
     brutalizing divisions
     the means (however improbable)

to overcome them
     The top *1 percent*
     gained over a trillion dollars

in the past dozen years
     as a result of tax breaks
     A wealth tax could retrieve that   Zinn '96 72

Or a statute could set (as I heard
     from an ex-bank executive
     citing an ex-Nixon aide)   Phillips

a managerial salary cap
     of say no more than thirty times
     the lowest wage of an employee

When *globalization arguments*
   insist on the unregulable nature
  of all social policy

in a world without economic borders
   this is manifestly untrue   *Saul 178: MacGregor '98 182*
  I don't grasp the details

but can see how the post-Enlightenment
   has used the words *social science*
  to separate economics

from considerations of *value*
   the root word oikonomia
  "the management of a household's

valuable assets"
   with a sense of prudent
  husbandry for the future

pushed aside by the economists'
   preoccupation with markets
  and the exchange mechanisms

for maximizing return   *Greider '97 458: cf. Daly and Cobb 138*
   we need to think of economics
  in the perspective of death

as did Hölderlin *the more*
   horses a man puts to his carriage
  the more he hides himself in gold

the deeper is the grave
   which he has dug for himself
  in which he lies as a living corpse   *Hölderlin '52 22*

The Greek and Jewish epics
   in contrast to texts
  which have forgotten the wisdom

known only from defeat
        remember not just the greatness
    but the fallibility of their heroes

who are punished for their excesses
        and loss of self-restraint
    ἀμείνω δ᾽ ἀΐσιμα πάντα   *Odyssey 7.310*

measure in things is best
        said the king to Odysseus
    like all Greeks the offspring

of pirates and captive women
        and when the minstrel celebrated
    how Greeks *wasted the lofty city*   *Odyssey 8.516*

Odysseus *let fall pitiful tears*   *Odyssey 8.531*
        as a woman wails
    and clings to her dying husband

while the enemy with their lances
        beat her back and shoulders
    and then lead her away   *Odyssey 8.523–28*

only after this weeping
        did he first identify himself   *Odyssey 9.19*
    and recall his woeful homecoming

how *he slew the Ciconian men*
        and took their wives and treasure   *Odyssey 9.37, 39–41*
    his many sorrows after that

from the old heroic excesses
        when *the men are slain*
    the city wasted by fire

and the children and women led away   *Iliad 9.593–94*
        Sorrows still follow excess
    the art of living together

obliterated by achievements
      measure in things is best
  the belief of the Phaiakians

who failed at the old heroics
      were good only at   *dance and* song   *Odyssey 8.253*
  the belief of the Founding Fathers

a truism so clichéd
      none of our present rulers
  seem even to think of it

now that the White House
      is less a place
  of human decisions

than a representation
      of what we carry around
  in our pockets

on the back of a twenty dollar bill

IV.v

In Siam after the war
      when the Buddhist *sangha*
  had lost control of *education and culture*   *Sulak '92 4*

(says Sulak's *Seeds of Peace*
      here on the library shelf
  my first night at the Villa Serbelloni)

the forces of Pridi   *Pridi Banomyong*
      who *wanted Siam to be democratic*   *Sulak '92 15*
  were ousted by Pibul   *Pibulsongkram*

whose racial vision for Thailand
        at the expense of non-Thais
    in alliance with Japan

Mussolini and Hitler
        whose writings he had translated   Sulak '92 157
    had led to Pibul's being tried

as a war criminal   Sulak '92 16–19
        and of course the Americans
    who during the Second World War

had been allied with Pridi
        preferred in the Cold War fifties
    to work with Pibul

just as in the Philippines
        the guerrillas who had fought the Japanese
    and turned in their names for veterans' benefits

were instead hunted down and murdered   McClintock 97
        CIA aid for Thailand
    was channeled through a front established

by a CIA agent   Marshall Scott & Hunter 32, 64
        with underworld bank connections   Scott and Marshall 92
    thus helping to open up the world

to a flood of heroin through Thailand   McCoy 168–73, 184–86
        while the mob in Manila
    helped to Westernize the Philippines

by its control of gambling   Seagrave 161–64, 328–37
        and later child prostitution
    carried on in the big hotels   Seagrave 318–23

Can we be surprised this happened
        when the mob was being protected
    both by Hoover in the FBI   Gentry 531–32

and Angleton in the CIA
>who *vetoed* a Justice Department investigation   *Scelso 168*
>and almost no one in the U.S. seemed to care

at least in its universities
>When I wanted to pinpoint
>the center of the corruption

I did not point to the CIA
>who seemed to think they were doing their job
>or even the government

which has always been corrupt
>so much as to universities
>for having sanctioned this system

And for what? Should we simply accept
>that (as the court historian
>Nebrija wrote in his dedication

to Queen Isabella of Spain)
>*language is the instrument of empire?*   *Rafael 23*
>I ask these questions

not out of hopelessness
>but pondering my own role
>and that of those I trusted

in today's *cunning of reason*   *Hegel '75B 89*
>When the Thai student
>supporters of democracy were slaughtered

by the Army in '76
>their teacher Sulak Sivaraksa
>whose book *Questioning Development*

was the outcome of meetings
>at the Villa Serbelloni   *Sulak '98 98*
>and whose work for *conservation and peace*

had for years it now turns out
      been supported by the CIA   *Sulak '98 87*
  (but then the CIA helped so many

from Frantz Fanon to the AFSC   *American Friends Service Committee*
      thus even my first book)   *Schurmann Scott & Zelnik*
Sulak came as an exiled scholar

for a year to UC Berkeley   *Sulak '98 149*
     where he quoted from the Suttas   *Sutras (in Pali)*
If people are mindful

using enlightenment as guidelines
    they can achieve the desirable society   *Sulak '92 110*
to support his own teaching

It is easy to hate our enemies
    who exploit us and pollute our atmosphere
But one must come to see

that there is no "other"
    It is greed hatred and delusion
that we need to overcome   *Sulak '92 116*

(Buddhist Economics
    which might have been called *Christian*
  but then *no one would have read it*)   *Schumacher; Ellsberg 389*

like the Torah provision for *Shemittah*   *release; Deut. 15:1*
    every seventh year
releasing the poor from their debts

and in *this year of jubilee*   *Levit. 25:13*
    the return of all leases to the Lord   *Levit. 25:10, 23*
the moralization of property   *Heine; Humash 533*

an economics of freedom
    (only when the state is well-tempered
can there be a well-tempered psyche

no security from wealth
        can match that when none is poor)
    an economics practiced now

by the staff at the soup kitchen
        as opposed to that of the system
    ("the management of assets"

pushed aside by the economists'
        preoccupation with markets)   *Greider '97 458; cf. Daly and Cobb 138*
    the commodification of liberty

into choices of channels
        colas political parties
    overseas Hiltons

The importance here
        is not whether Sulak's NGOs   *Non-Governmental Organizations*
    will outlast the Thai dictators

he himself felt his role
        in his *organization*
    on alternative development

had been a failure   *Sulak '98 156–57*
        it is that this critic
    from the other side of the world

seeking spiritual economics
        in a secular society
    along with his *friends*

like Abdurrahman Wahid of Indonesia   *Sulak '98 158*
        a more subtle utopian
    (who to my surprise

after the above was written
        will in time for the year 2000
    be elected Chief of State)

has spoken not just my beliefs
　　　　but for all of Wordsworth's
　　great family of poets　　　　　　　　　　　　*Prelude 11.62*

even the saints
　　　　Saint Francis Gandhi Weil
　　collected by Dan's son Robert　　　　　　　　*Ellsberg*

whose unanimity
needs again to be heard

IV.vi

The Emperor Frederick II
　　　　stupor mundi the wonder of the world
　　fluent in six languages

friend of the philosophers
　　　　whether Christian Muslim or Jew　　　　*Bury 165*
　　hoping to build *a single state*

by cancelling the power of the Popes　　　　　*Bury 164*
　　chose to defy his excommunication
　　under a fatal illusion

of his own power　　　　　　　　　　　　　　*Bury 157*
　　　　he *banished all friars*
　　ordered his subjects to capture

prelates journeying to the council　　　　　　*Bury 156*
　　but by his ambitions brought about
　　the virtual dissolution of the Empire　　　　*Bury 165*

and the liberation of the Italian middle class
　　　　what he had least intended
　　This humbling of secular power

(the pain of Henry
  wandering at Canossa)   *Hölderlin '84 102–03*
    reinforced by the dedication

of the new mendicant orders
      was in a pallid way repeated
  with the collapse of Richard Nixon

whose war with the media
    who *decide what Americans will learn*   *Lucas 271*
  led to his humiliation

The key to the hegemony
      of Western secular power
  has been its continuous challenge

by more cautious restraints
      from what Coleridge and Eliot
  looked to as a clerisy

but the successful Watergate coalition
      of press lords the FBI and CIA
  was no clerisy

and even if Nixon's hope to establish
      within the White House
  his own intelligence agency   *Epstein '77 229–32*

could be seen like Frederick's
      hegemonic aspirations
  a threat to all

what survived was rather
      an intensification
  of invisible and irresponsible power

Can there be a clerisy
      with churches drifting apart
  colleges lost in their committeework

the left restricting itself
  to innovation
  the right to conservation?

And what of the poets?
    Nadezhda Mandelstam
  survived the Soviet terror

by her sustaining faith
    in *the work of the poet*
    as vehicle of world harmony   *Mandelstam 225; Heaney '95 193*

Heaney wrote of *poetry's function*
    as an agent of possible transformation   *Heaney '95 114–15*
  providing *foreknowledge*

of certain things which
    we already seem to be remembering   *Heaney '95 159*
  inserting himself

into a grand tradition
    Virgil's prophetic
    impose law with peace   *pacique imponere morem; Aeneid 6.852*

Dante's *hard enigma*
    of the giant slain   *Purgatorio 33.43–50*
  Milton's prediction *we no more shall need*

the regal scepter   *Paradise Lost 3.340*
    (language inspiring the middle class
  that brought forth the American Republic)

Yeats' *great Memory*
    that renews the world   *Yeats '68 79*
  But how many poets alive besides himself

can Heaney point to? his last example
    is Elizabeth Bishop
  and what shall we say of Bishop's eye

so finely focused with the sandpiper's
  to the millions of quartz grains on the beach
  in a world of mist   *Bishop '67 113; Heaney '95 175–76*

and so slanted in Brazil
  at the time of the '64 coup
  by her chance friendship with Lacerda   *Carlos Lacerda*

one of the chief conspirators
  When she wrote that *this time*
  Goulart finally went too far

and was deposed in *forty-eight hours*
  by *a few brave generals*   *Bishop '94 424–25*
  she may well not have known

of the coup plotters
  in the U.S. Embassy
  of the U.S Marines offshore

to lend courage to the Army
  of the thousands thrown in jail
  like Luiz Alberto working with Freire   *Luiz Alberto Gomez de Souza,*
                                                Paulo Freire

for *conscientização*   *consciousness-raising*
  all this might have seemed to her
  a world of mist

but then why did she write to her friend
  don't believe Le Monde
  which suspected the U.S. oil companies

or that *the victory parade*
  was quite spontaneous   *Bishop '94 425*
  when in fact it was one of many

carefully planned for months
  by a U.S. priest?
  And why do I pick on Bishop

when we have seen MacDiarmid
          embrace *the Cheka's horrors*   *Heaney '95 118*
     Borges the Argentine generals

or Neruda Stalin
          Heaney was there in the room
     when the Chilean poet

who had also been imprisoned
          praised Neruda's love of freedom
     for which the Ukrainian poet

denounced her with heartfelt passion
          Askold who brought us there   *Askold Melnyczuk*
     has lauded Milosz

What is poetry which does not save
          nations or people?   *Milosz 78*
     before noting his silence

about *the forced resettlement*
          of a quarter of a million Ukrainians
     in 1947   *Melnyczuk 4–5; cf. Nahaylo 17*

while those who committed most
          in the Blakean challenge
     to build Jerusalem

first Yeats and above all Pound
          overvexed by the stress
     of trying to integrate

a world that is insane
          lapsed like Blake himself
     from the strength of their passions

into specious hatreds
          of invented enemies
     I am making so much of this

needing to realize
    there is no clerisy of poets
  in an age striving to believe

that poetry *makes nothing happen*   Auden 197
    (a quietism which challenges
  without any mind to

Shelley's conviction that poets
    whatever their actual beliefs
  advance the interests of Liberty)   Shelley '20 30

truth emerges
    from letting go
  of the need for poetic Truth

Heaney was quite right
    to find Bishop *transformative*
  in *the redress of poetry*   Heaney '95 168

for her *peculiar honest gaze*   Heaney '95 181
    those poets Wordsworth aspired to
  as *each with each connected*   Prelude 12.301–02

were mostly dead   being
    like the priests in *Utopia*
  saintly

and therefore very few   More 83

IV.vii

Let others debate the canon!
    I who mostly escaped
  a classical education

187

reading Ovid and Dante for myself
    heard them as counselors
  to mistrust the constructed world

as in Isaiah's
    She that was full of justice
  righteousness lodged in her—

but now murderers!   *Isaiah 1:21*
    or Virgil's rebuke of *frenzy*   *belli rabies et amor habendi;*
  of war and passion for gain   *Aeneid 8.327*

or Augustine *what are states*
    when they lack justice
  if not organized crime?   *latrocinia; Aug. City of God 4.4*

or in the early days
    when it was still lonely
  to oppose the Vietnam War

there was John Adams *a nation*
    at *height of power*
  never fails to loose

her Wisdom and Moderation   *Adams '62 4.158*
    to say nothing of Jesus
  the prime talking-point of charlatans

and Grand Inquisitors
    For what are we profited
  if we gain the whole world

and lose our own soul?   *Matthew 16:26*
    and his first community
  the primitive church

who *had all things in common*   *Acts 4:32*
    Saint Martin who provoked
  the Emperor's anger

by his vain attempt
> to prevent a heretic's death   *Sulp. Sev. Dial. 2.12; Hoare 133–37*
> Saint Francis Xavier in the east

who condemned the brutal greed
> of the Portuguese
> while de las Casas in the West

for some reason not canonized
> condemned *the cruel and inhuman*
> *treatment of the Spaniards*

against a *peaceable people*
> *many buried alive*   *Chomsky '93 198–99*
> Looking for whistle-blowers

I tracked down the witness
> to the Albigensian Crusade
> who revealed how northerners

entered the city of Béziers
> *killed almost all the inhabitants*
> *from the youngest to the oldest*   *Historia Albigensis 50*

the Abbot urging *Kill them all*
> *the Lord knows who are his own*   *Dialogus Miraculorum 5.21*
> only to find all this approved

as a *miracle*
> by the papal legates   *Patrologia Latina 216.137–41;*
> Well! no tradition is perfect   *Historia Albigensis 292*

which is why we need a canon
> to give preference to Milton's
> *by things deemed meek*

subverting worldly strong   *Paradise Lost 12.566–67*
> One might have hoped
> that with the passage of centuries

wisdom might be received
        more and more easily
    but it is not so

the universities themselves
        are busy disenthroning
    what the past accepted

reading *the literary work*
        as an ideological production   *Eagleton 85*
    instead of with Benjamin

no document of civilization
        which is not at the same time
    a document of barbarism   *Benjamin '68 256*

many books I used to teach
        like Sulpicius Severus or the Grettissaga
    are out of print

and apart from a few icons
        like the Bible and Shakespeare
    publishers make their fortunes

from new books not old ones
        blockbusters promising breakthroughs
    like that *sensational best seller*   *Newsweek 4/12/48 51*

the Kinsey Report
        with its misleading claim
    which offended me for years

to present an *objective*
        body of fact about sex   *Kinsey 5-8; J. Jones 518*
    rather than a sermon

on highly debatable matters   *Trilling 462; J. Jones 587*
        from one who *loathed*
    Victorian morality   *J. Jones xii*

Unaware until now
      he *had been badly injured*
      by sexual repression   *J. Jones xii*

from a dominating father
      and unaware of motives
      fathered within my own family

with its bibles from Russell and Krafft-Ebing
      I wrote how Kinsey had died
      after masochistic excesses

and how he had participated
      in licentious parties
      with Hitler's convicted publicist   *Lee 105*

misreading his book as a case
      for emancipation through indulgence
      rather than for tolerance

most sexual activities
      would become comprehensible
      if we knew *the background*

of each other's behavior   *J. Jones 532*
      I wanted two things
      difficult to reconcile

mystery   openness
      A son of the Enlightenment   *J. Jones 532*
      Kinsey wanted openness

by abolishing mystery
      But openness unguided
      led to anomie not freedom

I remember Berkeley
      in the 1970s
      those of us in our midst

who believed with Kinsey himself
    under proper circumstances
    pedophilia could be beneficial   *J. Jones 512*

mistrusting all restraints
    as impediments to joy
    With Lenin so crudely demonized

by cops and hypocrites
    we did not waste time considering
    if he had not in fact been dangerously

wrong to separate
    the necessities of today
    from the freedom promised tomorrow

the man to come
    parted as by a gulph
    from him who had been   *Prelude 11.59–60*

a split which in retrospect
    seems not unlike Kinsey's
    born from that sense of *crisis*

which impelled my father in the '30s
    myself in the '60s
    and which has been traced from Rousseau   *Sluga 24–25, 263*

(to see *one's own time*
    as the one-time basic
    revolutionary moment of history

is *one of the most destructive*
    habits of modern thought   *Foucault '89 251; Sluga 74*
    said Foucault   which is true

if we mean by *revolution*
    a social lobotomy
    and not its original sense

of a *turning* or *conversion*
    we being a people
  both *wounded by*
wirklichkeitswund

and seeking reality
    in a perpetual crisis
  the state of emergency
und Wirklichkeit suchend
Celan 35; Carson 94

not the exception
    but the rule)
  There has to be two of me!
Benjamin '68 257

one part welcoming our spread
    out into illogic
  the wealth of reality

to which we surrender ourselves
    the sheer awesomeness
  of our electronic possibility
Auerbach '57 488
http://www.alltheweb.com

for semiotic freedom
    and disintegration into darkness
  before our world

may be unified once again
    one part of me relieved
  this poem has worked back to

the one *Serat* or Way
    so many ancestors describe
  our radical past
Acts 9:2; Confucius Daxue i;
Digha Nikaya 19.8

the end nothing else
    but to seek out the lost mind
  that enables ruptures
Mencius 6A:11.4

revolution (a turning forward)
    and conversion (*tshuvah*
  repentance or turning back)
repentance; turning to God

We can see both
       (when not blinded by the denial
    we rely on to survive)

as faces of the same deep
       mundane necessity
    nothing more radical

close dangerous   than this
       in the face of death
       (*Wo Gefahr ist*   *Where danger is*

wächst das Rettende auch)   *grows also what saves; Hölderlin '52 216*
       that we *love one another*   *John 15:12; cf. Leviticus 19:18*
    for which *you must change your life!*   *Rilke 61*

we must change the world

IV.viii

To Fred Crews

When I read of Russell's
       war to the knife
    between intellect and intuition

opposing Bergson who *thinks*
       the intellect a wicked imp
    and *loves instinct*   *Monk 235*

was I wrong Fred to think of you?
       And why did I so react
    to your demeaning of Yeats' *voice*

of the revolt of the soul
       against the intellect
    where I saw Yeats following Shelley   *Yeats '86 303; Murphy 373;*
                                                              cf. Yeats '68 65–66

194

(*the imagination*
  has some way of lighting on the truth
  that the reason has not)   Yeats '68 65

but where you heard *a mere echo*
  of a far more confident voice
  Madame Blavatsky?   Crews '96 26; cf. Murphy 372

Though I had to approve
  your dislike of charlatans
  this struck me as a reduction

Surely we both admire Forster
  for letting Adela in the cave
  glimpse (as you wrote

in your balanced essay)
  an *order of truth beyond*
  the field of her rational vision   Crews '62 161

(a depth you saw also in Hawthorne
  a more penetrating fiction
  than any slice of life)   Crews '66 263

just as Russell admitted
  what he had learnt from Shelley   Monk 34
  two levels *one of science*

another terrifying subterranean
  which in some sense held more truth
  than the everyday view   Monk 317

bonding him to Conrad
  both men sharing with Freud
  the ever-imminent danger

of sinking into the madness
  below the civilised crust   Monk 320
  both men pulling back like Marlow

195

from the edge of the fire
          at *The Heart of Darkness*   *Monk 317*
     (Even you who once

continued to body-surf
          while the two helicopters
     searched for the drowned man

have in your own way tested
          the limits of safety)   *cf. Monk 317*
     When I first wrote you to defend

Yeats' use of intuition
          I had in mind
     his repetition from Shelley

before his involvement
          in the Irish troubles
     had shattered his dreams

for want of correspondence
          with the imagination
     the rich have become richer

the poor poorer
          from an unmitigated exercise
     of the calculating faculty   *Shelley 1887 30–31; Yeats '68 68*

(a passage so relevant
     ,   to our mental plight today
     it is not in the Cambridge Edition)   *cf. Shelley 1975 609*

but in our disagreement
          I see that I overreacted
     when I wrote of *a landscape torched*

by relentless demands
          for *the needed evidence*   *Crews '98 xxiii*
     which critics like Popper

have used to liberate us
from Hegel Marx
and moralists back to Plato

whereas most of our actual torchings
are done in the name of faith
by those who think themselves moral

My citation of Popper
was for that campaign
he himself called a *war effort*   *Cockett 82; MacGregor '98 32*

Your citation of Popper   *Crews '95 8*
was for his critique
of the self-validating

both of us agree with
and I share your respect
for *the rational-empirical ethos*   *Crews '95 8*

so it was gratuitous of me
to hunt for deeper meanings
in your scathing metaphors

like your dismissal of Freud
as a *visionary artist*   *Crews '95 12*
who *stood to his patients' dreams*

more as painter to his pigments
than as sleuth to his cigar ash   *Cioffi 110; Crews '95 11*
or to invoke Wittgenstein

for interpreting Freud
as a matter of *a good simile*   *Cioffi 105*
Indeed it is obvious

there is a *Yeats problem*   *Crews '96 29*
when sotted by Blavatsky   *Bloom 70, 75, 410*
as well as the hatreds

swirling round him in Ireland   *Bloom 318–24*
      Yeats obsessed with the *antithetical*   *Bloom 279, 318*
while voicing the despair

and powerlessness we all must feel
      in a demonic century
turned even on Shelley

whose *logical* efforts
      to satisfy desire   *Yeats '68 421*
      Yeats blamed for the *Jacobin frenzies* *Yeats '68 425*

of those round him like Maud Gonne   *Bloom 307*
      saying now *we must not demand*
even the welfare of the human race   *Yeats '68 425*

so I have to examine
      what issue inside myself
made me challenge you

I suspect that it had to do
      with my fear late last night
that I myself lacked madness

(*the ferocity that is needed*
      to redeem culture)   *Monk 353–54*
which produced a vivid dream

of descent from Mount Royal
      down a rotting staircase
into a private estate

of nineteenth-century gardens   *(Garsington?)*
      I had no business in
from which *both asleep and awake*   *Yeats '68 159, 423*

I then recovered
      what I was tempted wrongly to call
a *repressed memory*

that had somehow escaped
        my dredgings these sixteen years
    the undergraduate night

I alone in the basement
        of the McGill Union
    facing the arrival

of a woman no longer loved
        my Rhodes application late
    heard on the telephone

a landlord threatening to sue
        I who before then
    had occasionally heard voices

natter within me
        now listened to them
    screaming incomprehensibly

in a way which brought strangers
        to lift me off the floor
    my muscles unmanageable

and for the next four years
        I waited grimly
    for it to happen again

as it did at Oxford
        after I failed my degree
    only this time those who held me

were my roommates and friends
        the long fear mostly over
    I still wish to preserve the distinction

between those who think mostly in words
        and those who think images
    that cannot be put into words

they make themselves manifest   Wittgenstein 6.521; Monk 568
        from the Buddha to Wittgenstein   Majjhima Nikaya 592
    the flowing forms of mind

freed from all impulse
        not out of itself   Yeats '68 75
    I had hoped we both might share

in Flaubert's fantasy
        mystical in the last analysis
    but like all true mysticism

based upon reason and experience
        of a self-forgetful absorption
    in the subjects of reality   Auerbach '57 429

But your talents are better employed
        exposing how Freud's views
    on *the return of the repressed*   Crews '95 168

have been used to support
        a *plague of false charges*
    in that *highly lucrative enterprise*

the recovered memory business   Crews '95 242, 194
        One should hardly need to say this
    but from every point of view

(except perhaps that of the crayfish
        we plucked with twigs
    from a stream behind Big Sur

and dropped into sizzling butter)
        you are *a kind and gentle man*   Begley 29; Crews '95 293
    having somehow learned

more than either Russell or Yeats
        the habits of sanity
    which in a world ill-governed

are not always to be condemned   Milosz and Scott 17

Imagination!
      source of language!
    reflection of language!

enlarging not by yourself
      but as language escaping
    the rules of syntax

prosody aesthetics
      dialectically enlarges
    from Virgil's strict similes of control

Neptune calming the ocean
      like an orator a crowd   *Aeneid 1.142–53*
    even Hades a place

of measured judgment
      to Ovid's *discors concordia*   *discordant harmony; Met. 1.433*
    in which those too fixed

on order or even music
      Pentheus Orpheus
    are torn apart by the chthonic

forces they fail to respect   *Ovid Met. 3.712–33; 11.1–43*
      and those too devoted
    to what the young Keats called

the holiness of the Heart's affections   *Letters 11/22/1817*
      Myrrha Narcissus
    suffer the terrible

retribution of what they wished   *Ovid Met. 10.460–87, 3.478–90*
      And in the Dark Ages
    the image became a symbol

as the world retreated from cities
        and syntax became more loose
    what once were similes

obscured into mysteries
        Dido as wounded deer   *Aeneid 4.69*
    confounded with the hart

panting among water brooks   *Psalm 42:1*
        or Audradus   the twofold moon
    part dark part changing to light

a figure of Easter and ourselves   *Audradus; Patrologia Latina 115.23B*
        all books all nature a text
    inspired by a single Author

Whether one sees this
        as progress towards realism
    or towards surrealism

two innovations which have now
        like all before them
    both shrunk into genres

with the maturation
        of language itself
    along with art and music

inevitably there emerge
        patterns whose fulfilment
    not visible until much later

embraces Blake Balzac
        or even in our own time
    language or computer poets

Poets Laureate rappers Hallmark poets
        all of them no matter what they say
    in their outward performance

still guided from within
>by something   what is it?
>not the Ich but an Ungenannt   *Unnamed*

Freud never mentioned?
>our entropic society
>always diffusing writers

into a kind of ocean
>to the point where imagination
>by filling every cranny of the mind

with truth and its opposite—lies
>has become a fetish
>in the cult of Imagination

the virtuoso croaking
>*of shivering frogs*
>*despairing in their swamp*   *Nietzsche '87 #809*

self exfoliating to Self
>enlightenment to Enlightenment
>as *civilization progresses*

accumulating its pyramiding memories
>(the Web by which moments ago
>I called up the text of Audradus

from Perth in Western Australia)   *http://tobruk.library.uwa.edu.au*
>*its mountain of statistics*
>*which is finally the Tower of Babel*   *Williamson 140*

Imagination! I had believed you
>on the chosen authority
>of Dante Wordsworth and Shelley

as the strongest redress
>to the debasing influence
>*of the calculating faculty*   *Shelley '87 30–31; Yeats '68 68*

but whatever has moved
  me to write this poem
has pushed me to your limits

your overgrowth
  of proliferating foliage
that to our detriment

has obscured the trunk beneath
  The workings of dialectic!
Thus if the adult Keats (*the poetical*

character has no self)   *Letters 11/27/1818*
  anticipated Eliot
  the progress of an artist

is a continual extinction
  of personality   *Eliot '51 17*
Eliot moved still further

challenging the fetish
  that *pursuit of self-knowledge*
  will come upon

a self that is universal   *Eliot '51 27*
  with the insistence
  that the poet must develop

the consciousness of the past   *Eliot '51 17*
  a nostalgia for wholeness
from Nietzsche to Yeats

rejecting political forms
  that had proven to work badly
for idealized alternatives

that proved to work even worse
  Eliot's pseudo-royalism
  an innocent affair

compared to those ersatz Wholes
        invoked by Heidegger and others
    to create a spiritual world   *Sluga 3*

As if like ourselves
        so also *language*
    had to go through

the thousand darknesses
        of deathbringing talk
    to come back to light "enriched"   *Celan 34; Carson 29*

Amazed at this process
        we all are part of
    I see now that Popper

had good reason to rebut
        the uses made of Hegel
    in the German 1930s   *Sluga 69, 106, etc.*

as much as I myself
        had good reason to react
    against the Popperian clichés

about *social engineering*
        that were laid on us at Oxford
    I feel the tug of two forces

the yang of experiment
        (was Dahmer's imagination
    of eating his sexual victims

fed first from literature?)
        the yin of intuitive retreat
    to this impersonal movement

that like a crystal expanding
        into a hyperconcentrated solution
    creates its own structure

and just as significantly
       its own dissolutions
    until without knowing it

(the hermeneutical experience
       an activity of the thing itself
    an event that happens to one)   *Gadamer 465*

I find myself facing
       the aporias and dilemmas
    of texts I had never read

like Heidegger's lecture
       while sporting a swastika   *Wright 166*
    in which poetry is not

the *Ausdruck von Erlebnissen*   *Heidegger '80 26*
       the expression of inner experiences   *cf. Hölderlin '22 222–24;*
    but *the concentration*   *Hölderlin '88 138–40*

by which one *reaches down*
       into the ground of existence   *Heidegger '80 8; Wright 169*
    providing the opportunity

for *a true collection*
       of each individual
    into a Gemeinschaft   *original community; Heidegger '80 8; Wright 169*

not a nationalist *Volk*
       as Heidegger imagined
    but that global community

we all are part of
       the dead
    who *can save the living*   *Carson 95*

(when we hear them clearly
       in our moments of loss)
    since we have been

a conversation   Hölderlin '52 178
        transmuting *the world into word*   Heidegger '49 279
    all of us fashioned

by something   what is it?
from the shards of shattered genres

                        IV.x

Intuition!
        the way forward
        from the way back

in an effort to reconcile
        the hard Odyssean *nostos*   *voyage home*
    of rigorous self-restraint

past the Sirens' song of *what happens*   *Odyssey 12.191; Horkheimer*
        and the soft Orphic descent   *and Adorno 32*
    into self-remembrance

turning back his longing eyes   *Metamorphoses 10.57*
        to the lost love of his past
    (the memory-work

that follows political failure)
        Dante like Saint Augustine
    had a clear knowledge

of where to get to—
        knowledge leading to love
    in the enjoyment of God

but we with no further goal
        than the ground we stand on
    are focused on this path

already under foot
             which is a plebeian one
        for anyone wishing it

no more than the proper
             recognition and tracing of despair
        at the *reasonableness*

of a world ill-governed
             where even in America we die
        from polluted aquifers   Harr

and a path of healing
             by which gravity
        could become its opposite

by converting shadows
             into language
        even a *happiness*

from *hap* and *mishap*
             fitting not to ourselves
        but to *the music of what happens*   Heaney '98 173

the needs without and within
             until this earth we stand on
        is first an Underworld

of the chattering dead
             whose Tartarean waters
        still carry *innumerable*

headless bodies   Colombian Bulletin, Spring '97, 21
             human life itself *a shadow*   Euripides Medea 1224; Hegel '77 122
        and when this seems absolute

intellect battling against faith
             everything *shattered to atoms*
        language *a broken utterance*   Hegel '77 328; Goldmann 6–7

all history leading

      from the slingshot to the megaton bomb   *Adorno 320*

   and then in the post-catastrophic

pleasure of survival

      the spring trees crowding again

   like children on the hillside

each one with its different

      fresh shade of green

   we stare at more intensely

for the sake of a dead friend

      as we return to the breath

   the inner remembrance

of how to enjoy this life   *cf. Habermas '79*

      the mystical word enjoyment

   as much as enmindment

needed to bring to focus

      fei yang   *fei yin*   *not yang*   *not yin; Zhuangzi 22*

   the scattered traces

from which we cannot make

      a coherent *picture*   *Hegel '77 328; Goldmann 7*

   We imagine the Many

we intuit the One

      the center not in ourselves

   but in *what happens*

the needs of language emerging

      both to and from us

   in faith that to comprehend

(intuition!

      when all things have spread apart

   what flows back in!)

is to love this fallen earth
           as just now at the Villa Serbelloni
      and the mountains of Lake Como

*(the same delicious lake
           where art and Nature mixed*   *Prelude 6.604, 634, 657*
      Wordsworth looked down on)

dinner on the terrace
           *(how this common life
      gets channeled there*

into orders of columns)   *Montale 215*
           waiting for the eclipsed moon
      while being served by Muslim

Sri Lankan waiters from Milan
           who understand why Ronna is fasting   *on Yom Kippur*
      and are devotees of cricket

Luiz Alberto good-humoredly   *Luiz Alberto Gomez de Souza*
           recalling from his detention
      after the coup in Brazil

his memory of order
           as it works today in a top-down
      globalized world

the interrogator's cheery
           Let us dialogue together
      and on the desk the black

rubber club stamped *Dialogue!*
           and then the five Chinese scholars
      singing us a translated

Mongolian folksong
           of love under a full moon
      And we marvel at this luck

this happiness of the present
the *profane perfection of mankind*   Yeats '89 326; Heaney '95 159

IV.xi

In the Bishop's Palace in Oporto
           overlooking the old port
     on the river Douro

with its huge advertisements for port
           Graham Dow the same Scots
     families as in India and Montreal

where we all spoke on East Timor
           including the leader
     of a Muslim student group from Indonesia

facing possible imprisonment
           when he went back home
     George Aditjondro (already

banished from his country   *Indonesia*
           his passport invalidated
     for defending East Timor

and showing how Indonesia's wealth
           was not so much Chinese
     as concentrated in the hands

of a tiny clique
           surrounding Soeharto)   *Jakarta Post 8/14/98*
     the Argentinian lawyer

who in the time of the generals
           spoke for the mothers of the *desaparacidos*
     and most dramatically

X the East Timorese
        whose own risk on her return
    was not arrest but disappearance

and who against the advice
        of her friend Professor Barbedo
    told the group how she had been raped

I finally met Max Lane
        the translator of Pramoedya
        Indonesia's greatest living writer

often mentioned as a candidate
        for the Nobel Prize for literature   *Washington Post 6/7/98*
    and I said to him *Pramoedya*

is so original
        even the reviewers who praise him   *New Yorker 5/27/96*
    are too Western in their outlook

to follow what he has done
        for the genre of the novel
    at the end of the Buru Quartet

and Max replied *He will never*
        be given a Nobel
    all of the current writers

flourishing under Soeharto
        are dead set against it
    Of course I thought

you cannot be powerful in a state
        and unlike it in character   *Plato Gorgias 513B*
    Thus Pramoedya was thrown in prison

first by the Dutch
        for championing independence   *Pramoedya '99 194*
    then by Sukarno's Army

for challenging the treatment of Chinese Pramoedya '99 330
     and then for fourteen years without trial
  by Soeharto's New Order

while until recently
     students were tortured and imprisoned
  for sharing his books

When asked to apologize
     Pramoedya   a meditator
  (the sound of your breath

a form of samadhi)   *Pramoedya '99 302–03*
     wrote the following
  I myself am Javanese

I was educated to Javanese ideals
     guided by the Mahabharata
  at whose climax they bathe

in the blood of their own brothers
     while other peoples who
  have managed to slip their shackles

are the nations that rule the world
     Even in the belly of Dutch power
  Java still glorified

its Kampung culture   *narrow world-view*
     they bathed in the blood of their brothers
  right up through 1966

And because Java was no longer
     in the belly of European power
  the slaughter reached an unlimited scale

without colonization my country
     would have ceaselessly spilled
  the blood of its sons and daughters

cultural integrity   a bogey
        for the countries stuffed with capital
    by which free peoples are enslaved

the unemployed become murderers
        vast forests are torn apart
    It is necessary that I emphasize

the problem of power
        that tends to turn people into bandits
    above all if they have held it for decades

and without ever knowing Verlichting   *Enlightenment (Dutch)*
        Aufklaerung   remain in thrall   *Enlightenment (German)*
    to Kampung culture

which at any time
        can explode without notification
    Once more—my apologies   *Pramoedya '92*

And now with Soeharto gone
        one reads Pramoedya in the pages
    of the *Washington Post*

as well as the *Jakarta Post*
        still looking to *a generation*
    whose hands are not bloody

and whose mouths have not been soiled
        by the government's cakes   *Washington Post 6/7/98*
    But the PRD leaders he respects   *People's Democratic Party*

are still in jail
        and the most powerful voices
    denouncing the recent murders

and rapes of the Chinese
        are the top Muslim leaders
    like Abdurrahman Wahid

third-generation
      leader of NU   *Nahdlatul Ulama*
   the largest non-governmental Islamic

organization in the world   *Ramage 45*
      not even in Saudi Arabia
   do they have a mass Muslim organization

The government there will not allow it   *Ramage 215*
   who in May in Surabaya   *1998*
organized a meeting of one million

from all over East Java
   all dressed in white
to stop the fomenting of hatred

against the Christian Chinese
   by the more reactionary
clerics in his own NU

from the *pesantren*   *Islamic boarding schools*
   some of whose youth in '65
were brought in by Army trucks

to kill the secular teachers
   and send their corpses
down the river Brantas   *Pipit Rochijat 43–44*

but which Sulak now praises
   for wanting *development*
from the grass-roots up   *Sulak '97 82*

Gus Dur was educated   *Abdurrahman Wahid*
   in the West as well as Islam
like Habibie who in a few months

will do what we never expected
   let East Timor go free
and if we now visit Java

it should not be for shadow plays
            or the Buddhas of Borobodur
    but to learn whether a moderate

Muslim like Gus Dur
            who to everyone's surprise
    in time for the year 2000

has become the new Chief of State
            and who *still suffers nightmares*
    from the NU's involvement

in the 1965 massacre   *L.A. Times 2/10/2000*
            can in a coalition
    with extremists and the military

while still beholden to the IMF
            (which *has allowed Indonesia*
    to continue heavy subsidies

on food and fuel)   *NYT 4/8/98; Washington Post 12/30/98*
            achieve the tolerance
    of the Panca Sila   *Five Principles*

(*religious   not secular*
            though not based
    on any particular faith)   *Ramage 12*

these hopes for Indonesia
being also our own

                    IV.xii

                October 31, 1997

Intuition!
            the gateway to the terrifying
    unity of God!

the problem of evil
        not frightening   to be solved
      the problem of God   insoluble

The poet who honestly seeks
        this unity all-pervading
      may well be torn limb from limb

if not sunk in fury
        at the world's recalcitrance
      but in the search for peace

we can still take guidance
        from our Orphic experience
      increasingly passionate

Odysseus sailing after knowledge
        dug an elbow-deep pit   *Odyssey 11.25*
      and would not talk to his mother

until after he had learned
        from the blind seer Teiresias
      to *wish to curb his spirit*   *Odyssey 11.105*

where Aeneas going deeper
        into the mental darkness
      of his previous failures

(in *the Orphic effort*
        to haul life back up the slope)   *Heaney '95 158*
      wept on meeting Dido's ghost   *Aeneid 6.475–76*

the tears that it is said
        he had failed to weep before Dido   *Aeneid 4.449*
      when pleading his *case*   *Aeneid 4.337*

while Dante deeper still
        near the center of the earth
      when invited to weep

at the fate of Ugolino
      cursed all Pisa and its children
until the sight of Beatrice

Inferno 33.42
Inferno 33.79–90

released from his frozen heart
      a great deluge of tears
leading him up to God

Purgatorio 30.97–99
Augustine Conf. 8.12.18

God who is everywhere
      but not in equal measure
This earthway is anyone's

Paradiso 1.3

each one of us may confess
      I am unclean in the midst
of a people of unclean lips

Isaiah 6:5

as it befell Ezra Pound
      caged in sight of Ugolino's tower
his eyes streaming from the dust

facing *the loneliness of death*
      and seeking *the cause in himself*
to confront the memory of Margaret

Cantos 82/527
Cantos 77/468
Margaret Cravens d. 1912
Carpenter 155, 180–81, 194

who had *entered the lotus*
      when *pity melted her heart*
thus he confessed in his own fashion

Cantos 77/471
Awoi; Pound '70 331

whether for self or humankind
      les larmes que j'ai creées m'inondent
(*the tears I have made are drowning me*)

Cantos 81/521
Cantos 80/513

and by his awareness
      that these tears had brought him
al som de l'escalina

to the summit of the stairway;
Cantos 84/539; Purgatorio 26.148

he moved *with the seed's breath*
      the mist or *chi* on the mountain
that heals by night

Cantos 83/531

what has been done by day   *Mencius 2A:2.15*
        an earthly ascent in time
    towards what is already here

intelligence!   Twofold
        both what there is to be known
    and the power to know it   *American Heritage Dictionary*

the mysterious correspondence
        (as in biblical typology)
    unresolved by Aristotle   *d. 322 B.C.E.*

Arabs like Ibn-Rushd   *Averroes d. 1198 C.E.*
    or Schoolmen like Aquinas   *d. 1274 C.E.*
    between active and passive intellect   *Aristotle De Anima 3.5*

or ourselves and God   *Purgatorio 25.73*
        God of the blue jay   *Aphelocoma coerulescens*
    through the yellow mustard patch   *Brassica nigra*

God who has brought us to compassion
        and to corpses in rivers   *P.D.Scott '89 25; P.D.Scott '92 55*
    God whose declining dharma   *mo fa*

will reveal like the waning moon
        as our shadow moves across it
    the outline of its fullness

God before whom
        we stand alone
    till the time when God's failure helps *Hölderlin '14 4.147; Heidegger '49 265*

so that we can see the world
        both as Saint Bennet did
    the size of a *walnut*

*gathered within the ray
        of a single sunbeam*   *Greg. Dial. 2.35, 4.7;*
    and also as Orpheus   *Paradiso 22.137*

immersed from love in the redeeming
    stink of earth
      the passions of destruction

which at times overwhelm us
      being also from God
    this earthway is everyone's

in the chaos of the present
        from our place in time
    not yet to be decoded

· is the tao of all dharmas
      from the brookside wren
      in its burst of *nibbana*-chatter   *Nirvana (Pali); enlightenment*

to the reconciled
      Colonian chorus saying
      all these things are well ordained   *Sophocles Oed. Col. 1779; Heidegger '49 361*

to the Yuba City Prune Festival
      a cornucopia
    of quilts corn dogs jalapeño jellies

where as the ungainly
      teen-age chorus sings
    she's our tootsie-wootsie

the consummate ten-year-old
      ballerina pirouettes
    with a white parasol

her studied downward smile eluding time

THIRD RETREAT:
BELL-RINGING IN YUCCA VALLEY

1

The woman cabbie who drives us
down through Morongo Valley
used to be a bar-tender
I learned to work only
where there was recreation
like golf or a swimming pool
never where men came together
only to drink
In the end I gave it up
because of the money
one place the woman before me
had to lie on the floor
while the robber shot out the mirrors
and the whiskey bottles

I used to meditate too
my father who died when I was fifteen
learned it from Norman Vincent Peale

At seventy miles per hour
the cushion on which I sit
recedes from the *chi* of the earth
and from the *chi* of the air
as we enter the narrow valley
out of the desert into Los Angeles
in which rank after silent rank
of tall spare windmills
idle
witnesses to what the roadsign
warns us of: a region
of high winds

2

Hard to believe
at 4:45 this morning
in the desert moonlight
I'm striking a heavy bell-shaped
slab of bronze
with half a stick
Across the desert valley
a dog barking
as if aroused by this
clear humming which travels farther
now that I have learned
to strike more deliberately
and less often

Yesterday when I spoke
for the first controlled minute
with the stranger who had sat beside me
through ten days of silence
I wanted to say *What a waste*
of this gift that joins us!
how sad that people
chatter continuously
without this silence
that allows us to feel the
vibrancy of words

An hour earlier when I learned
my count was a day off
this was indeed the end
I went back to the silent
meditation hall

and heaved as I had so often
great silent sobs
not so much from the loss
as out of the fullness
I must now abandon

3

The crying came
only at the good times
as when Ronna reached out
and held me to her body
or the night of the full moon
two passover candles in the desert
dining room
the woman from India
picking up the parsley
and reading thoughtfully the instructions
before dipping it
into the salt water
to remind us all of tears

4

The bad times
I was far too out of touch
with my earthly body
for anything like tears
already the first day
my mind like a zoo
with the cage doors all open
for the boring animals
but it was in the night
when for the fourth time
counting three from the last retreat
someone stepped on me
gently not like that first bonecrusher
arousing again inside me
the three-year-old child
furious not just at the offense
but at the teacher
unable to stop such things

I lay awake that night
convinced I would have to leave
this pack of undisciplined
self-serving children
too old to be stepped on
persuaded even it was Ronna
(*who cares if she is put off*
that I'll never sit again?)
and not my own karma
that had got me into this

5

A fortunate fall?
In five days that three-year-old
grew to be eight
as hindrance after hindrance
traced back to childish fear
my need to speak well
to my dharma teacher
at risk to honesty
from the need of an only child
to please grown-ups
like my need to cry out
after the crash of china
at the washing-table
I didn't do it!
the clear memory
of having done something wrong
in the nursery classroom
with Lepage's Paste
though water-soluble my fault
was serious: it prevented
me from advancing
to the next step
less impermanent
Lepage's Glue

6

The last two nights
a hypnagogic spectacular
continuous auroras
of fear-ridden images
which the sixty-eight-year old
had the pleasure of explaining
to his eight-year-old parent

the beautiful pear opening
to reveal at the center
of its firm white flesh
two squirming bristly-haired
grubs that would bite you
if you did not quickly let go

and instead of saying simply
as James our teacher had advised
Aversion aversion
(*the word* Why? *is dangerous*)
the sixty-eight-year-old said *See!*
you have always been scared
of getting close to anything
to which you are attracted

It went on all night
I did not even want to sleep
so rare was this opportunity
to see in front of my eyes
the road so rotten at first
with half-thawed ice and mud
we could make no progress
legs sinking in deeper
both of us terrified
for a moment until the older
one remembered *Nothing*
is permanent   all things change
and explained to the eight-year-old

his old preference for icy
surfaces that did not threaten

as the road emerged
to a relief the dry
sands of the desert
what seemed like an oasis
of thick-trunked palms
proved to be a place
(like this Institute we had rented
once vigorous now a relic)
of departed energy
where absurd dying men
exercised vainly on upside-down
stationary bicycles
to elude death
and then the beautiful
desert again
going on and on

endless

7

The joshua trees
do not bury their dead

in the daytime they touch
unrotting trunks with their shadows

in the nighttime they stand alone
indistinguishable

from the yogis among them
standing immobile

at rest from their walking meditation
under the stars

8

Having until now
back in Berkeley

(Ronna at *tahara*
the funeral rite

of washing the body
of a widow and friend

we know from the synagogue)
written not one word

it is hard now to recapture
so far from those passages of breath

and walking slowly
foot up foot down

the moment   how I came
to the breakfast table

and silently placed
my ginger tea

in a blue china cup
next to an orange

orange

9

In the same moment I remembered
something less:

that was how I learned color
and indeed abstraction

an orange is orange
(something at the bottom

of each year's Christmas stocking
and later in my nursery-book

translated from the French
about an orangerie

the dark green leaves
more oranges in them than I

a young boy in Montreal
had ever seen)

my teacher Jack responded:
Couldn't you write poems

that are a selfless
poetry of objects

like Ponge?
(leaving me to ponder

between objects and Buddha-mind)
and that night the teacher Carol:

the winds of change
blow over emptiness

who can they harm?

10

The moon that last night
beginning to wane

rose after the end
of the final sitting

I looked to the west
and with the bird glasses

I was not supposed to use
examined the long tail

of the comet Hale-Bopp
descending towards the snow-capped

Mount Gorgonio
Forgive me! I knew

this was the last time
I would see it so clearly

for four thousand years

V

太 極

TAI JI—THE GREAT ORIGIN

"That which lets now the dark, now the light appear, is tao."
—*I Ching* 1.319

"Night is as clear as day
The darkness and light to thee are both alike."
—Psalm 139:10–11

"The dissonances of the world are like the quarrels of lovers.
Reconciliation exists in the midst of strife, and everything that
is separated finds itself again."   —Hölderlin '48 236

"Whatever can be said at all can be said clearly; whereof one
cannot speak, thereon must one be silent."   —Wittgenstein

V.i

To Ronna

After the cherubim
>of the Spinozan intellect
>Dante reached the seraphim of love   *Paradiso 28.72*

who were in that small-looking space
>between the knowledge of God
>and God

but you have taught me
>it is too easy
>to love what will never hurt us

we are made for this world
>*when we love there will be pain*
>which we do not flee from

there being no gift more precious
>than an opened heart
>From *ladies who have intelligence of love*   *Vita Nuova 19*

I once learned a sweetness
>I saw again just last night
>the innocence in the face

of the child violist
>wholly focused on the music
>her eyes transmitted to her hands

the *insegnamento* of grace
>from instincts not yet too corrupted
>by the pain of life

the love exalted by Dante

was unconsummated two-dimensional
tangential to daily life
his Beatrice survived by dying

what use was knowledge of that love
to Milton's first marriage
or T.S. Eliot's?

So from love *at one with reason*   *Vita Nuova 2*
(but not with the world)
the Elizabethans and Romantics

turned to its opposite
rejecting the stairway to heaven
in favor of this life

they explored the grandeur
of love as obsession
the kind of headline-maker

that leads from opera
to bad Hollywood movies
as if this were progress

and not a return to the passion
the Buddha warns against
I cannot claim total ignorance

of desires which shamed me
even as I surrendered to them
(my wild eye fixed

on the gold slipper above me
riding like a chariot of fear)
or of sweet pleasures

234

which seemed to cost nothing
          except an almost imperceptible
     hardening of the heart

but none of these emotions
          ever shook up my life
     and went to its very core

as does sheer being with you
          at first your close eye
     for the details of life

which could set us both laughing
          then those secrets just for ourselves
     not to be shared

about which I will only say
          some of them are like a furnace
     a smelter in which rare metals are refined

so intense you must forgive me
          for the dross which sometimes
     surfaces in my heated speech

and other times more mundane
          just now in the breakfast nook
     slicing the ginger root

for your cup of fresh tea
          or coming to you last night
     standing face to face

to have my collar buttoned
          still others more elevated
     like the view down from the Monte di Nava

to our windows in the Villa Serbelloni
          and then that dark month
     after your brother died

(compared to which loss the fire
         where you lost all your possessions
      was a mere bonfire)

I knew then there were parts of you
         no man will ever understand
      but I have no need to

you have taught me to listen
         to the emotions which rest on my heart
      like the hushed mists

hanging over this dark September lake
         and to that ever-present friend the breath
      the quiet inward seashore

to which we both listen
         on our journey into the earth
      from which there is no return

we are more mindful of each other
         because mindful of that darkness
      let me say to the Suttas   *Sutras (in Pali)*

that opening my heart this way
         is like entering the Stream   *Buddha path*
      what has emerged besides pain

in these four years
         since you lost your brother
      cousins uncles father

is a love facing death
         not just remembering death
      when I stood on two rocks

and could not drain the half-submerged canoe
         saying *I'm too old for this*
      I saw in your tears the courage

236

it must have taken
>to marry someone older
>I listen to your heart

resolutely counting the seconds
>for both of us
>an incarnation

of the First Noble Truth
>*love opening hearts to joy*
>*opens them also to pain*

the unloved never experience
>for which they are not to be envied
>each halting increase

in trust for each other
>(and from which we gain strength
>to engage the world

the art of the impossible)
>increases also the risk
>sometimes almost to the verge

of excruciation
>the check to the breath
>I remember on the sheer cliff

fingers and cheek on a cleft
>as I a reckless eighteen-year-old
>summoned the courage to drop

back to the unseen narrow ledge below me
>or failing that to the bottom
>with its four white crosses in a row

the world seeming at an end
>I had never before felt
>so concentratedly alive

as again now unable to imagine
living without you

V.ii

Having reached the too narrow balcony
        up the perilous fire escape
    I stand up naked

my heart clutched with the great height
        and I say to the woman who brought me here
    as part of the experiment

It is discomforting to have learned
        they have found DNA on Mars
    it is too much for my mental world

at this point my dark glasses
        fall down nine stories to the earth
    I call out to the stranger *Those are mine*

and having thus dangerously
        exposed my nakedness
    I wake up   to see at once

√ this is my inadequacy
        as the poem begins to finish
    getting nowhere final

it is as if you
        who in the dream were silent
    were in fact speaking *We*

are still with you
        over your head
    often perhaps reflecting

what was already on my mind
        but in some dreams more
    a rebuke to what is happening

or a surprise   like that ghost
        revenant from my childhood terror
    words writing themselves

the way humans make history
        not just as they choose
    (Bloch: *The work of art*

a star of anticipation
        on the way home through darkness   *Bloch 151*
    through the linear *ordo seclorum*

the *ordo* of return
        to the *long sought after homeland*)
    but compounded from the past

original   *the primary form*
        from which varieties arise   *AHD*
    and *authentic*   *having an undisputed origin*   *AHD*

(before these two words
        like our word *author*
    moved from Creator to Self)

as if sometimes it is the dead
        who do the talking
    just as a dream is said to be from God   *Iliad 1.63*

and is not truly ours
        when I first invoked you   *P.D.Scott '89 10*
    I was exalted by despair

in a time like Wordsworth's
        exhausted by excess
        possessed by defamation   *Coleridge 87*

239

and the mess of my own life
    just as now the sleeplessness
  of my wakeful heart

(overwhelmed with the wealth
    of a life outwardly secure
  and inwardly perilous

from the guilt and fear of privilege
    it sees now throughout our dreams)
  leads to plain words *in prose*   *Williams 176, Chaucer 228*

which can be taken as a gift
    though God knows I and the reader
  have worked hard to reach this place

Subjectivity   the dialogue
    between the thalamus and cortex   *Seabrook 65*
  (the neurons replying to the senses

I dream   therefore I am)   *Seabrook 65*
    so that inner and outer enlightenment
  depend on each other

both of them lost
    when they are not *dialogical*
  and impious Greek arts   *Virgil Aeneid 2.106,152.163,195*

are pitched against blind
    superstitious Trojan furor   *Virgil Aeneid 2.244*
  this is what is wrong

with secular capitalism
    and its mimetic offspring
  secular communism

facing *the theocratic alternative*   *Said '93 305: cf. Benjamin '78 312*
  of *shariah* and *jihad*   *Islamic law: Muslim holy war*
    (proposed to Edward Said

at Cairo University
      by *a well-spoken woman whose head*
    was covered by a veil)　　　　　　　　　　*Said '93 305*

I have written what I have seen
      for this unextraordinary millennium
    like every other year

an end and a beginning
      between the cosmic cycles　　　　　　　　*shemittot*
    of *din* judgment

and of *chesed*　　　　loving-kindness
      a kind of golden age　　　　　　　*Scholem 121*
    yang　　　　　comprehension

the strength not just to understand
      but to change the world
    (the fault of Enlightenment

like that of religion before it
      was that it changed
    not so much but so little

of our still mysterious world)
      tempered by yin　　　　compassion
    toward the Open

the Rebbe: *these words*
      shall be on your heart　　　　　　*cf. Deut. 6:6*
    and when your heart is broken

they will fall in
      the poetry of that lake
    was in the ruins

from Theodelinda's castle　　　　*Queen of Lombards d. 591 C.E.*
      to the empty walls of households
    rubble from so many failed dreams

that it is less a pain
        than an entry into fellowship
    to contemplate our own

and when Ronna and I danced
        naked in the middle of the night
    on the moonlit balcony

overlooking the lake
        more dreamlike even than the dream
    I felt like crying *May everyone*

experience such breathing
        moments   this
   now

already gone

V.iii

To language and humans
        endlessly
    redefining each other

in an orbic space-time
        where the East lies west of the West
    and the myth of the past before us

as the fullness of noon
        is the beginning of nightfall
    so darkness of experience

is the beginning of insight
        happiness makes us forget
    so the surfeit of knowledge

points towards that horizon
          between the body *on earth*
     and the mind *in heaven*

the earthway
          where we struggle to discover
     what has always been known

FOURTH RETREAT
WALKING AT SPIRIT ROCK

For Marie and Jack

DAY NINE

The hours pass under my feet
another year gone round the corner

as the water-spider
with efficient forestrokes

keeps skating upstream
against the current

DAY THIRTEEN

big mind   small mind
only to the stranger

looking down from above
one shoe on each bank of the brook

does it appear
he is getting nowhere

DAY FIFTEEN

Ryokan: *By not knowing
we enter the Way*

DAY SIXTEEN

How did you come like this
to walk on water?

AFTERWORD BY THE AUTHOR

Almost twenty years ago, in 1980, I began, without realizing it, the trilogy *Seculum*. The initial draft of the first volume, *Coming to Jakarta: A Poem About Terror* (published 1988), was completed in six weeks, in healing response to a personal crisis, after a publisher suppressed a prose book of mine about the JFK assassination that was already in page proofs for a print run of 250,000 copies. *Jakarta* began with a diffuse sense of nausea and terror, but quickly defined a focus: my stifling inability to dispel by prose the widespread denial of U.S. involvement in the 1965 Indonesian army massacre of leftists, when more than a half million people were killed. Soon however I was looking at the same process of denial in myself: I had once discounted my own university's support of elements working with the army. In this way *Jakarta* took the form of an argument, at first with the external world, but increasingly with myself.

In the eight years it took me to complete and publish *Jakarta*, I found that I could not bring it to closure until I had embarked on an unplanned sequel, *Listening to the Candle*. (My wife laughs at *Candle*'s subtitle, "A Poem on Impulse," since it was composed over ten years, before being published in 1992.) A poem of penumbras and shadows, *Candle* became a corrective contrast to the worldly purposiveness and pessimism of *Jakarta*, which came more and more to strike me as poetically one-sided. So *Candle* began by exploring inner, aesthetic, and personal experience; as it progressed it moved into a more deeply spiritual and explicitly Buddhist perspective.

This left me with an even more acute problem of closure than I had with *Jakarta*. I now had two parts of a whole whose movements and directions were almost antithetical, each negat-ing the attempted holism of the other. Thus I could not close the pages of *Candle* until I had committed myself to a third volume. (At the time, I could visual-ize no more than the three opening sections.)

This third volume of *Seculum* incorporates both the secular yang elements of the first (dedicated to my father the rationalist reformer) and the spiritual yin elements of the second (dedicated to my mother the Nietzschean artist). *Minding the Darkness* contains a yang followed by a yin movement, although these are presented like day and night, each arising out of and evolving into the other. (My father was also a poet, and my mother was known as an intellectual painter.)

In this way *Minding the Darkness* has emerged as an effort to recon-cile the movements of secular (historical) enlightenment, and of spiri-tual (personal) enlightenment, that are represented by the first two volumes. It attempts to comprehend the deep antinomies that have characterized our culture: Apollo and Dionysus, Greek and Hebrew, Platonism and empiricism, Classical and Romantic, intellect and love.

Like other long poems by older men (I am now over seventy), it toys dangerously with abstract didactic impulses. At the end it sug-gests with Shelley that both outer enlightenment (the current word is development) and inner enlightenment are damned, even murderous, if they do not honor each other.

ii

In 1980-81 I produced my first working draft of *Coming to Jakarta* in about six weeks. By contrast, after I began *Minding the Darkness* in 1991, it was years before both the style and the ultimate direction of the poem defined themselves. A tracing back of my own discontents made me more and more aware (especially in *Darkness*) of my enmesh-ment in the mental issues of this century. What I struggled with had invariably been struggled with before, whether by authors like Hölderlin I had not looked at for decades, or by authors I had hardly glanced at at all (such as Wittgenstein or Benjamin). Moreover, I be-came increasingly conscious of emergent changes in both the concerns and the tone of the poem through the decade it took me to write it.

Thus there is a double chronology in the work (not unlike that in Wordsworth's *Prelude*): underneath the not-very-clear time sequence of the surface narrative lies the divergent time sequence of composition. In a work searching for original mind, the under-sequence is perhaps the true narrative development.

There follow, below, the dates of each section for the reader interested in the time-sequence of the poem's composition. It should be understood however that each date corresponds only to the first composition of a section. Every section was edited and often recast over the years. Thus the date is a *terminus a quo,* not *ad quem*—a date of initiation rather than of completion. There are sections in which there are events or sidenotes more recent than the date at the beginning, and even sections, e.g. III.v, where the writing interacts with the narrative described. As the later sections emerged in a style that was increasingly alien to that of the outset, it became necessary to close the poem, and the trilogy, before all of the earlier sections had been completely overwritten.

(Here, then, are the dates for each section: Part I—I.i, 11/5/91; I.ii, 11/12/91; I.iii, 12/21/91; Part II—II.i, 2/15/94; II.ii, 9/8/97; II.iii, 6/2/94; II.iv, 2/21/94; II.v, 3/90; II.vi, 2/19/94; II.vii, 8/5/94; II.viii, 2/15/95; II.ix, 10/22/97; II.x, 4/14/95; II.xi, 8/21/95; II.xii, 10/21/93; First Retreat, 12/95; Part III—III.i, 7/14/98; III.ii, 11/24/95; III.iii, 5/15/95; III.iv, 2/27/96; III.v, 4/15/95; III.vi, 12/24/95; III.vii, 9/19/95; III.viii, 4/9/96; III.ix, 9/7/97; III.x, 11/6/98; III.xi, 9/8/94; III.xii, 6/9/96; Second Retreat, 8/96; Part IV—IV.i, 2/2/97; IV.ii, 4/12/97; IV.iii, 3/2/97; IV.iv, 6/12/97; IV.v, 10/4/97; IV.vi, 10/6/97; IV.vii, 10/10/97; IV.viii, 12/19/96; IV.ix, 10/9/97; IV.x, 10/10/97; IV.xi, 8/21/98; IV.xii, 10/31/97; Third Retreat, 4/97; Part V—V.i, 1/1/97; V.ii, 9/30/97; V.iii, 1/3/97; Fourth Retreat, 2/20/99.)

The poem's open-ended engagement with historical process led to some surprises with aesthetic consequences. As originally written, the section on East Timor (IV.xi) had no idea of East Timor's imminent liberation. Still less, when writing about Abdurrahman Wahid, a cleric at that time unknown in the West, did I suspect that events would turn me, improbably, into a eulogist for a head of state.

BIBLIOGRAPHY

Adams, John, ed. Charles Francis Adams. *Works*. Boston: Little, Brown, 1856.

Adams, John, ed. L. H. Butterfield. *Diary and Autobiography*. Cambridge, MA: Belknap Press, 1962.

Adams, John, and Thomas Jefferson. *The Adams-Jefferson Letters. The Complete Correspondence Between Thomas Jefferson and Abigail and John Adams*. Chapel Hill, NC: University of North Carolina Press, 1959. Vol. I.

Adler, Rachel. *Jewish Bulletin of Northern California*, 9/2/94, 1A.

Adorno, Theodor W., trans. E.B. Ashton. *Negative Dialectics*. New York: Seabury Press, 1973.

Agee, Philip. *Inside the Company: CIA Diary*. Harmondsworth: Penguin, 1975.

AHD: *American Heritage Dictionary of the English Language*. New York: American Heritage Publishing, 1969.

Auden, W.H., ed. Edward Mendelson. *Collected Poems*. New York: Random House, 1976.

Audradus Senonensis. *De Fonte Vitae*. In J.-P. Migne. *Patrologia Latina*, Vol 115, 18–24.

Auerbach, Erich. *Mimesis: The Representation of Reality in Western Literature*. Garden City, NY: Doubleday Anchor, 1957.

Auerbach, Erich, trans. M. and E.W. Said. "Philology and *Weltliteratur*." *Centennial Review* 13 (1969), 1–17.

Baldwin, James. *The Fire Next Time*. New York: Dial Press, 1963.

Beard, Charles, and Mary Beard. *The Making of American Civilization*. New York: Macmillan, 1937.

Becker, Carl L. *The Heavenly City of the Eighteenth Century Philosophers*. New Haven: Yale UP, 1932.

Begley, Adam. "Terminating Analysis." *Lingua Franca*, 4 (July/August 1994), 24–30.

Benjamin, Walter, ed. Hannah Arendt. *Illuminations*. New York: Schocken Books, 1968.

Benjamin, Walter, ed. Peter Demetz. *Reflections: Essays, Aphorisms, Autobiographical Writings*. New York: Schocken Books, 1978.

Benjamin, Walter, edited and annotated by Gershom Scholem and Theodor W. Adorno. *The Correspondence of Walter Benjamin, 1910–1940*. Chicago: University of Chicago Press, 1995.

Bishop, Elizabeth. *Selected Poems*. London: Chatto & Windus, 1967.

Bishop, Elizabeth, ed. Robert Giroux. *One Art: Letters*. New York: Farrar Straus & Giroux, 1994.

Bloch, Ernst. *Geist der Utopie*. Frankfurt: Suhrkamp Verlag, 1964.

Bloom, Harold. *Yeats*. Oxford: Oxford UP, 1970.

Bodhidharma, trans. Red Pine. *The Zen Teaching of Bodhidharma*. San Francisco: North Point, 1989.

Brinton, Crane. *The Anatomy of Revolution*. New York: Vintage, [1938] 1965.

Brown, Peter. *Augustine of Hippo: A Biography*. Berkeley and Los Angeles: University of California Press, 1969.

Brzezinski, Zbigniew. *Power and Principle*. New York: Farrar, Straus & Giroux, 1983.

Bury, J.B., et al. *The Cambridge Medieval History,* ed. J.R. Tanner, C.W. Previte-Orton, and Z.N. Brooke. Volume VI: Victory of the Papacy. Cambridge: Cambridge UP, 1957.

Cadogan Guides: *Tuscany, Umbria and The Marches,* by Dana Facaros and Michael Pauls. London: Cadogan Books, 1995.

Carpenter, Humphrey. *A Serious Character: The Life of Ezra Pound*. Boston: Houghton Mifflin, 1988.

Carson, Anne. *Economy of the Unlost (Reading Simonides of Keos with Paul Celan)*. Princeton: Princeton UP, 1999.

Cavafy, Constantine, trans. Edmund Keeley and Philip Sherrard. *Collected Poems*. Princeton: Princeton UP, 1975.

Celan, Paul, trans. Rosmarie Waldrop. *Collected Prose*. Manchester: Carcanet, 1986.

Chan, Wing-tsit. *A Source Book in Chinese Philosophy*. Princeton: Princeton UP, 1963.

Chaucer, Geoffrey, ed. F.N. Robinson. *The Works of Geoffrey Chaucer*. Boston: Houghton Mifflin, 1957.

Chomsky, Noam. *Deterring Democracy*. New York: Hill & Wang, 1992.

Chomsky, Noam. *Year 501: The Conquest Continues*. Boston: South End Press, 1993.

Chomsky, Noam. *Keeping the Rabble at Bay: Interviews with David Barsamian*. Monroe, ME: Common Courage Press, 1994.

Chossudovsky, Michel. *The Globalisation of Poverty: Impacts of IMF and World Bank Reforms*. London: Zed Books, 1997.

Churchill, Ward. *A Little Matter of Genocide: Holocaust and Denial in the Americas, 1492 to the Present*. San Francisco: City Lights, 1997.

Cioffi, Frank. *Freud and the Question of Pseudoscience*. Chicago: Open Court, 1998.

Cockett, Richard. *Thinking the Unthinkable: Think-Tanks and the Economic Counter-revolution*. London: HarperCollins, 1994.

Coleridge, Samuel Taylor. *Biographia Literaria; or, Biographical Sketches of My Literary Life and Opinions*. London: George Bell, 1885.

Collier, Peter and David Horowitz. *Destructive Generation: Second Thoughts About the Sixties*. New York: Summit Books, 1989.

Crews, Frederick C. *E.M. Forster: The Perils of Humanism*. Princeton: Princeton UP, 1962.

Crews, Frederick C. *The Sins of the Fathers: Hawthorne's Psychological Themes*. New York, Oxford UP, 1966.

Crews, Frederick, et al. *The Memory Wars: Freud's Legacy in Dispute.* New York: New York Review Books, 1995.

Crews, Frederick. "The Consolation of Theosophy." *New York Review of Books,* 43, 14, September 19, 1996, 26–30.

Crews, Frederick C., ed. *Unauthorized Freud: Doubters Confront a Legend.* New York: Viking, 1998.

Daly, Herman E., and John B. Cobb, Jr. *For the Common Good: Redirecting the Economy Toward Community, the Environment, and a Sustainable Future.* Boston: Beacon Press, 1989.

Degler, Carl N. *Out of Our Past. The Forces That Shaped Modern America.* New York: Harper Colophon, 1984.

Demaris, Ovid. *Captive City.* New York: Pocket Books, 1970.

Dialogus Miraculorum: Caesarius of Heisterbach, trans. H. von E. Scott and C.C. Swinton Bland. *The Dialogue on Miracles,* London: George Routledge, 1929.

Digha Nikaya: *The Long Discourses of the Buddha: A Translation of the Digha Nikaya,* by Maurice Walshe. Boston: Wisdom Publications, 1987, 1995.

Dinnerstein, Leonard. *Antisemitism in America.* New York: Oxford UP, 1994.

Djwa, Sandra. *The Politics of the Imagination. A Life of F.R. Scott.* Toronto: McClelland & Stewart, 1987.

Dundes, Alan, ed. *The Blood Libel Legend: A Casebook in Anti-Semitic Folklore.* Madison, WI: University of Wisconsin Press, 1991.

Dunn, Lt.Col. William R. *"I Stand by Sand Creek:" A Defense of Colonel John M. Chivington and the Third Colorado Cavalry.* Ft. Collins, CO: Old Army Press, 1985.

Eagleton, Terry. *Criticism and Ideology: A Study in Marxist Literary Theory.* London: NLB, 1976.

Eliot, T.S. *The Use of Poetry and the Use of Criticism.* London: Faber, 1934.

Eliot, T.S. *Selected Essays.* London: Faber, 1951.

Ellis, Joseph J. *American Sphinx: The Character of Joseph Jefferson.* New York: Alfred A. Knopf, 1997.

Ellsberg, Robert. *All Saints: Daily Reflections on Saints, Prophets, and Witnesses for Our Time.* New York: Crossroad Publishing, 1997.

Epstein, Edward Jay. *Agency of Fear: Opiates and Political Power in America*. New York: G.P. Putnam's Sons, 1977.

Epstein, Edward Jay. *Deception. The Invisible War Between the KGB and the CIA*. New York: Simon and Schuster, 1989.

Fairburn: *Fairburn's Book of Crests of the Families of Great Britain and Ireland*. London: T.C. and E.C. Jack, 1905.

Farinelli, Arturo. *Dante e la Francia: dall' età media al secolo di Voltaire*. Geneva: Slatkine Reprints, 1971.

Ferris, Timothy. "Astronomical Notebook: Minds and Matter." *New Yorker*, May 15, 1995, 46-50.

Foucault, Michel. "Human Nature: Justice versus Power" [a debate with Noam Chomsky]. In *Reflexive Water: The Basic Concerns of Mankind*, ed. Fons Elders. London: Souvenir Press, 1974.

Foucault, Michel, trans. John Johnston. *Foucault Live (Interviews, 1966–84)*. New York: Semiotext(e), 1989.

Foucault, Michel, ed. Paul Rabinow. *The Foucault Reader*. New York: Pantheon, 1984.

Freed, Donald. *Plays*. New York: Broadway Play Publishing, 1990.

French, Peter J. *John Dee: The World of an Elizabethan Magus*. London: Routledge & Kegan Paul, 1972.

Frend, W.C.S. *The Donatist Church: A Movement of Protest in Roman North Africa*. Oxford: Clarendon, 1971.

Friedmann, Yohanan. *Shaykh Ahmad Sirhindi: An Outline of His Thought and a Study of His Image in the Eyes of Posterity*. Montreal: McGill-Queen's UP, 1971.

Gadamer, Hans-Georg. *Truth and Method*. New York: Continuum, 1995.

Gates, John Morgan. *Schoolbooks and Krags: The United States Army in the Philippines, 1898-1902*. Westport, CT: Greenwood Press, 1973.

Gentry, Curt. *J. Edgar Hoover: The Man and the Secrets*. New York: Penguin, 1991.

Godwin, Joscelyn. *The Theosophical Enlightenment*. Albany: State University of New York Press, 1994.

Goldman, Francisco. "Murder Comes for the Bishop." *New Yorker*, March 15, 1999, 60–77.

Goldmann, Lucien, trans. Henry Maas. *The Philosophy of En-*

lightenment: The Christian Burgess and the Enlightenment. London: Routledge & Kegan Paul, 1973.

Goodwyn, Lawrence. *Democratic Promise. The Populist Movement in America.* New York: Oxford UP, 1976.

Gregory I, Pope. *The Dialogues of Saint Gregory, Surnamed the Great.* London, P. L. Warner, 1911.

Greider, William. *Secrets of the Temple: How the Federal Reserve Runs the Country.* New York: Simon and Schuster, 1987.

Greider, William. *One World, Ready or Not: The Manic Logic of Global Capitalism.* New York: Simon and Schuster, 1997.

Habermas, Jürgen, trans. T. McCarthy. *Communication and the Evolution of Society.* Boston: Beacon Press, 1979.

Habermas, Jürgen, trans. William Rehg. *Between Facts and Norms: Contributions to a Discourse Theory of Law and Democracy.* Cambridge, MA: MIT Press, 1996.

Harr, Jonathan. *A Civil Action.* New York: Random House, 1995.

Heaney, Seamus. *The Redress of Poetry.* New York: Farrar, Straus & Giroux, 1995.

Heaney, Seamus. *Opened Ground: Selected Poems 1966–1996.* New York: Farrar, Straus & Giroux, 1998.

Hegel, Georg Wilhelm Friedrich, ed. Hermann Glockner. *Sämtliche Werke,* Vol. XI. *Vorlesungen über die Philosophie der Geschichte.* Stuttgart: Fr. Frommanns Verlag, 1928.

Hegel, Georg Wilhelm Friedrich, trans. T.M. Knox. *The Philosophy of Right.* Oxford: Clarendon Press, 1942.

Hegel, Georg Wilhelm Friedrich, trans. William Wallace. *Logic: Being Part One of the Encyclopaedia of the Philosophical Sciences.* Oxford: Oxford UP, 1975.

Hegel, Georg Wilhelm Friedrich, trans. H.B. Nisbet. *Lecture on the Philosophy of World History.* Cambridge: Cambridge UP, 1975.

Hegel, Georg Wilhelm Friedrich, trans. A.V. Miller. *Phenomenology of Spirit.* Oxford: Clarendon Press, 1977.

Heidegger, Martin. *Existence and Being.* Chicago: Henry Regnery, 1949.

Heidegger, Martin. *Hölderlins Hymnen "Germanien" und "Der Rhein." Gesamtausgabe,* Vol. 39. Frankfurt: Klostermann, 1980.

Heidegger, Martin, trans. Richard Taft. *Kant and the Problem of Metaphysics*. Bloomington, IN: Indiana UP, 1990.

Heilbron, John. "Introductory Essay. I. Dee's Role in the Scientific Revolution." In *John Dee on Astronomy: Propaedeumata Aphoristica (1558 and 1568), Latin and English,* ed. and trans. Wayne Shumaker. Berkeley and Los Angeles: University of California Press, 1978.

Herder, Johann Gottfried, ed. Bernhard Suphan. *Herders Saemmtliche Werke*. Berlin: Weidmann, 1877–1913.

Historia Albigensis: Petrus Sarnensis, trans. W. A. and M. D. Sibly. *The History of the Albigensian Crusade,* Woodbridge, Suffolk: The Boydell Press, 1998.

Hoare, F. R., trans. *The Western Fathers*. New York: Harper Torchbooks, 1954.

Hölderlin, Friedrich, ed. Norbert von Hellingrath. *Sämtliche Werke*. Berlin: Propylaen-Verlag, 1914.

Hölderlin, Friedrich, ed. Erich Lichtenstein. *Briefe*. Weimar: Erich Lichtenstein Verlag, 1922.

Hölderlin, Friedrich, ed. Ernst Muller. *Hyperion; Empedokles*. Stuttgart: W. Kohlhammer, 1948.

Hölderlin, Friedrich, trans. Michael Hamburger. *Hölderlin: His Poems*. New York: Pantheon, 1952.

Hölderlin, Friedrich, trans. Richard Sieburth. *Hymns and Fragments*. Princeton: Princeton UP, 1984.

Hölderlin, Friedrich, trans. Thomas Pfau. *Essays and Letters on Theory*. Albany: State University of New York Press, 1988.

Hofstadter, Richard. *The Age of Reform; from Bryan to F. D. R.* New York: Alfred A. Knopf, 1955.

Hofstadter, Richard. "The Pseudo-Conservative Revolt— 1955." In Daniel Bell (ed.), *The Radical Right: The New American Right, Expanded and Updated*. Garden City, NY: Doubleday, 1963.

Hoig, Stan. *The Sand Creek Massacre*. Norman, OK: University of Oklahoma Press, 1977.

Horkheimer, Max and Theodor W. Adorno, trans. J. Cummings. *Dialectic of Enlightenment*. New York: Seabury Press, 1972.

Humash: Hertz, Dr. J.H. *The Pentateuch and Haftorahs: Hebrew*

Text, English Translation, and Commentary. London: Soncino Press, 1992 [A. H. 5752].

I Ching: *The I Ching or Book of Changes: The Richard Wilhelm Translation,* trans. Cary Baynes. Bollingen Series XIX. New York: Pantheon, 1950.

Jefferson, Thomas, ed. Paul Leicester Ford. *The Writings of Thomas Jefferson.* New York: G.P. Putnam's Sons, 1899.

Joachim of Flora. *Expositio in Apocalypsim.* Venice, 1517.

Joergensen, Giovanni. *San Francesco d'Assisi.* Rome: Francesco Ferrari, 1937.

Jones, A.H.M. *The Later Roman Empire, 284–602.* Oxford: Basil Blackwell, 1964.

Jones, James H. *Alfred C. Kinsey: A Public/Private Life.* New York: W.W. Norton, 1997.

Kant, Emmanuel. "What Is Enlightenment?" In *Kant's Political Writings,* ed. Hans Reiss, trans. H.B. Nisbet. Cambridge: Cambridge UP, 1970.

Karnow, Stanley. *In Our Image: America's Empire in the Philippines.* New York: Random House, 1989.

Kazin, Michael. *The Populist Persuasion: An American History.* New York: BasicBooks, 1995.

Kerkvliet, Benedict J. *The Huk Rebellion: A Study of Peasant Revolt in the Philippines.* Quezon City: New Day Publishers, 1979.

Kinsey, Alfred C., et al. *Sexual Behavior in the Human Male.* Philadelphia: W.B Saunders, 1948.

Klein, Rachel. "Shirine: A Thousand and One Nights." *Chicago Review* 44.1 (1998).

Kolko, Gabriel. *The Triumph of Conservatism: A Reinterpretation of American History, 1900-1916.* New York: Free Press of Glencoe, 1963.

Kolko, Gabriel. *Century of War: Politics, Conflict, and Society Since 1914.* New York: New Press, 1994.

Kytle, Calvin. *Gandhi, Soldier of Nonviolence: His Effect on India and the World Today.* New York, Grosset & Dunlap, 1969.

Lazaro de Aspurz, Padre, O.F.M. Cap. [Fr. Lazaro Iriarte, O.F.M.], trans. Patricia Ross. *Franciscan History: the Three Orders of St. Francis of Assisi.* Chicago: Franciscan Herald Press, 1982.

Lee, Martin A. *The Beast Reawakens*. Boston: Little, Brown, 1997.

Legge, James. *Confucius: Confucian Analects, The Great Learning and The Doctrine of the Mean*. New York: Dover, 1971.

Lilla, Mark. "The Riddle of Walter Benjamin." *New York Review of Books,* May 25, 1995.

Lucas, J. Anthony. *Nightmare: The Underside of the Nixon Years*. New York: Viking, 1976.

Luther, Martin, trans. Martin H. Bertram. *On the Jews and Their Lies*. In *Luther's Works,* Volume 47, *The Christian Society, IV*. Philadelphia: Fortress Press, 1955.

Luttwak, Edward. Comments in record of March 1983 National Defense University symposium on special operations. In Frank R. Barnett, B. Hugh Tovar, and Richard H. Shultz, eds., *Special Operations in U.S. Strategy*. Washington: National Defense University Press, 1984.

MacGregor, David. *The Communist Ideal in Hegel and Marx*. Toronto: University of Toronto Press, 1984.

MacGregor, David. *Hegel and Marx After the Fall of Communism*. Cardiff: University of Wales Press, 1998.

al-Maghut, Mohammed, trans. John Asfour. "The Tattoo." In Michael Harris, ed., *The Signal Anthology: Contemporary Canadian Poetry*. Montreal: Véhicule Press, 1993.

MacIntyre, Alasdair C. *After Virtue: A Study in Moral Theory*. Notre Dame, IN: University of Notre Dame Press, 1981.

Majjhima Nikaya: *The Middle Length Discourses of the Buddha: a New Translation of the Majjhima Nikaya,* trans. Bhikkhu Ñanamoli and Bhikkhu Bodhi. Boston: Wisdom, 1995.

Mandelstam, Nadezhda, trans. Max Hayward. *Hope Against Hope*. Harmondsworth: Penguin, 1975.

Mardock, Robert Winston. *The Reformers and the American Indian*. Columbia, MO: University of Missouri Press, 1971.

Marshall, Jonathan, Peter Dale Scott, and Jane Hunter. *The Iran-Contra Connection*. Boston: South End Press, 1987.

Marx, Karl, trans. Martin Nicolaus. *Grundrisse: Foundations of the Critique of Political Economy*. Harmondsworth: Penguin, 1973.

Marx, Karl, trans. Ben Fowkes. *Capital: A Critique of Political Economy,* Volume I. Harmondsworth: Penguin, 1976.

Mayer, Henry. *All on Fire: William Lloyd Garrison and the Abolition of Slavery*. New York: St. Martin's Press, 1998.

McClintock, Michael. *Instruments of Statecraft: U.S. Guerrilla Warfare, Counterinsurgency, and Counterterrorism*. New York: Pantheon, 1992.

McCoy, Alfred W. *The Politics of Heroin: CIA Complicity in the Global Drug Trade*. Brooklyn, NY: Lawrence Hill Books, 1991.

Melnyczuk, Askold. "Shadowboxing. Saved by Shame: Milosz's Concupiscent Curds." *Agni* 49 (1999), 1–10.

MEXI 7029. Mexico City CIA Station Cable of Nov. 23, 1963. National Archive Record No. #104-10015-10091.

Michelin Green Guide: *Tuscany*.

Miller, Stuart Creighton. *"Benevolent Assimilation": The American Conquest of the Philippines, 1899–1903*. New Haven: Yale UP, 1982.

Mills, James. *The Underground Empire: Where Crime and Governments Embrace*. New York: Dell, 1987.

Milosz, Czeslaw. *The Collected Poems 1931–1987*. New York: Ecco Press, 1988.

Milosz, Czeslaw, and Peter Dale Scott. "Translators' Note." In Zbigniew Herbert. *Selected Poems*. New York: Ecco, 1986.

Milton, John. *De Doctrina Christiana*. In *Complete Prose Works*, Vol. VI. New Haven: Yale UP, 1973.

Monk, Ray. *Bertrand Russell: The Spirit of Solitude, 1872–1921*. New York: The Free Press, 1996.

Montale, Eugenio, trans. Jonathan Galassi. *Collected Poems: 1920–1954*. New York: Farrar, Straus & Giroux, 1998.

More, Sir Thomas, trans. Robert M. Adams. *Utopia*. New York: Norton, 1975.

Mullins, Eustace Clarence. *A Study of the Federal Reserve*. New York: Kasper and Horton, 1952.

Murdoch, Iris. "Metaphysics and Ethics." Originally published in *The Nature of Metaphysics* (1957). Reprinted in *Iris Murdoch and the Search for Human Goodness*, ed. Maria Antonaccio and William Schweiker. Chicago: University of Chicago Press, 1996.

Murphy, William M. *Family Secrets: William Butler Yeats and His Relatives*. Syracuse: Syracuse UP, 1995.

Nahaylo, Bohdan. *The Ukrainian Resurgence*. Toronto: University of Toronto Press, 1999.

Nattier, Jan. *Once Upon a Future Time*. Berkeley: Asian Humanities Press, 1991.

Naylor, R.T. *Hot Money and the Politics of Debt*. New York: Linden Press/ Simon and Schuster, 1987.

Nietzsche, Friedrich Wilhelm, trans. Walter Kaufmann. *The Birth of Tragedy, and The Case of Wagner*. New York, Vintage Books, 1967.

Nietzsche, Friedrich Wilhelm, trans. Walter Kaufmann. *Ecce Homo*. New York, Vintage Books, 1969.

Nietzsche, Friedrich Wilhelm, trans. Walter Kaufmann. *The Will to Power*. New York, Random House, 1987.

Olson, Alan. *Hegel and the Spirit: Philosophy as Pneumatology*. Princeton: Princeton UP, 1992.

Paulinus of Pella. *Sancti Paulini Eucharisticon*. In Ausonius, Decimus Magnus, *Ausonius,* trans. Hugh G. Evelyn White, Vol. 2, 293–351. London, W. Heinemann; New York, G.P. Putnam's Sons, 1919–1921. Series title: Loeb classical library.

Phillips, Kevin P. *The Politics of Rich and Poor: Wealth and the American Electorate in the Reagan Aftermath*. New York: Random House, 1990.

Pinsky, Robert. *Poetry and the World*. New York: Ecco, 1988.

Pipit Rochijat. "Am I PKI or NON-PKI?" *Indonesia*, 40 (October 1985).

Poe, Edgar Allan. *Eureka: A Prose Poem: An Essay on the Material and Spiritual Universe*. San Francisco: Arion Press, 1991.

Popper, Sir Karl Raimund. *The Open Society and Its Enemies*. Princeton, Princeton UP, 1966.

Pound, Ezra. *Translations*. New York: New Directions, 1970.

Pound, Ezra. *Selected Prose 1909–1965*. New York: New Directions, 1973.

Pound, Ezra. *Cantos*. New York: New Directions, 1986.

Pramoedya Ananta Toer, trans. Max Lane. *This Earth of Mankind: A Novel*. New York: Penguin, 1981.

Pramoedya Ananta Toer, trans. Max Lane. *Child of All Nations*. New York: Penguin, 1996, 1990.

Pramoedya Ananta Toer, trans. Max Lane. *Footsteps*. Harmondsworth: Penguin, 1990.

Pramoedya Ananta Toer, trans. Alex G. Bardsley. *My Apologies, in the Name of Experience* [1992]. *Indonesia*, 61 (Spring 1996).

Pramoedya Ananta Toer, trans. Max Lane. *House of Glass: A Novel*. New York: W. Morrow, 1996.

Pramoedya Ananta Toer, trans. Willem Samuels. *The Mute's Soliloquy*. New York: Hyperion East, 1999.

Radu, Michael, and Vladimir Tismaneanu. *Latin American Revolutionaries: Groups, Goals, Methods*. Washington: Pergamon-Brassey's International Defense Publishers, 1990.

Rafael, Vicente L. *Contracting Colonialism: Translation and Christian Conversion in Tagalog Society under Early Spanish Rule*. Durham, NC: Duke UP, 1993.

Rahula, Walpola. *What the Buddha Taught*. New York: Grove Weidenfeld, 1974.

Ramage, Douglas E. *Politics in Indonesia: Democracy, Islam and the Ideology of Tolerance*. London and New York: Routledge, 1995.

Ranelagh, John. *The Agency: The Rise and Decline of the CIA*. New York: Simon and Schuster, 1986.

Remnick, David. "The Exile Returns." *New Yorker*, February 14, 1994.

Reston, James. *Last Apocalypse: Europe at the Year A.D. 1000*. New York: Doubleday, 1998.

Rilke, Rainer Maria, trans. Stephen Mitchell. *Selected Poetry*. New York: Random House, 1982.

Robson, Michael. *St. Francis of Assisi: The Legend and the Life*. London: Geoffrey Chapman, 1997.

Rorty, Richard. *Achieving Our Country: Leftist Thought in Twentieth-Century America*. Cambridge: Harvard UP, 1998.

Roth, Cecil. *History of the Jews in England*. Oxford: Clarendon Press, 1964.

Sachar, Abram Leon. *A History of the Jews*. New York: Alfred A. Knopf, 1965.

Safranski, Rudiger, trans. Ewald Osers. *Martin Heidegger: Between Good and Evil*. Cambridge, MA: Harvard UP, 1998.

Said, Edward. *The World, the Text, and the Critic*. Cambridge, MA: Harvard UP, 1983.

Said, Edward. *Culture and Imperialism*. New York: Alfred A. Knopf, 1993.

Saul, John Ralston. *The Unconscious Civilization*. Concord, Ont.: House of Anansi Press, 1995.

"Scelso, John" (former CIA intelligence officer). Testimony, in Hearing before the House Select Committee on Assassinations, Executive Session, May 16, 1978 (Secret). Partially declassified by the Assassination Records Review Board, October 1, 1996. National Archive Record No. 180-10131-10330.

Schlesinger, Arthur, Jr. *The Age of Jackson*. Boston, 1946.

Scholem, Gershon. *Kabbalah*. New York: Quadrangle/The New York Times Book Co., 1974.

Schumacher, E.F. "Economics as if People Mattered: An Interview with E.F. Schumacher." *Catholic Worker*, May 1977.

Schurmann, Franz, Peter Dale Scott, and Reginal Zelnik. *The Politics of Escalation in Vietnam*. New York: Fawcett, 1966.

Scott, F.R. *Collected Poems*. Toronto: McClelland & Stewart, 1981.

Scott, Peter Dale. "The Vietnam War and the CIA-Financial Complex." In Mark Selden, ed., *Remaking Asia*. New York: Pantheon, 1974.

Scott, Peter Dale. *Crime and Cover-Up: The CIA, the Mafia, and the Dallas-Watergate Connection*. Berkeley, CA: Westworks, 1977; Santa Barbara, CA: Open Archive Press, 1993.

Scott, Peter Dale. "The United States and the Overthrow of Sukarno, 1965-1967." *Pacific Affairs* (Vancouver, B.C.) 58.2 (Summer 1985), pp. 239-64.

Scott, Peter Dale. *Coming to Jakarta: A Poem About Terror*. Toronto: McClelland & Stewart, 1988; New York: New Directions, 1989.

Scott, Peter Dale. *Listening to the Candle: A Poem on Impulse*. Toronto: McClelland & Stewart, 1992; New York: New Directions, 1992.

Scott, Peter Dale. *Deep Politics II: Oswald, Mexico, and Cuba—The New Revelations in U.S. Government Files*. Grand Prairie, TX: JFK Lancer Productions and Publications, 1995.

Scott, Peter Dale. "Professor Peter Dale Scott's Letter to the ARRB [Assassination Records Review Board]." *Prevailing Winds* (Santa Barbara, CA), 3 [Spring 1996], 40-43.

Scott, Peter Dale, and Jonathan Marshall. *Cocaine Politics: Drugs, Armies and the CIA in Central America*. Berkeley and Los Angeles: University of California Press, 1991.

Seabrook, John. "Sleeping With the Baby." *New Yorker*, November 8, 1999, 56-65.

Seagrave, Sterling. *The Marcos Dynasty*. New York: Harper and Row, 1988.

Seferis, George. *Days of 1945–51; A Poet's Journal*. Cambridge, MA: Belknap Press of Harvard UP, 1974.

Sellers, Charles. *The Market Revolution: Jacksonian America, 1815–1846*. New York: Oxford UP, 1991.

Shelley, Percy Bysshe, ed. Ernest Rhys. *Essays and Letters*. London: Walter Scott, 1887.

Shelley, Percy Bysshe, ed. T. W. Rolleston. *A Philosophical View of Reform*. London: Humphrey Milford and Oxford UP, 1920.

Shelley, Percy Bysshe, ed. Newell F. Ford. *The Poetical Works*. Cambridge Edition. Boston: Houghton Mifflin, 1975.

Sidney, Philip. *Correspondence* (Letter of 18 October 1580). In *The Complete Works*, ed. Albert Feuillerat, Vol. 3. Cambridge: Cambridge UP, 1926.

Sluga, Hans. *Heidegger's Crisis: Philosophy and Politics in Nazi Germany*. Cambridge, MA: Harvard UP, 1993.

Snell, Bruno, trans. Thomas Rosenmeyer. *The Discovery of the Mind: The Greek Origins of European Thought*. New York: Harper and Row, 1960.

Sulak Sivaraksa. *Seeds of Peace. A Buddhist Vision for Renewing Society*. Berkeley: Parallax Press, 1992.

Sulak Sivaraksa. "Integrating Head and Heart: Indigenous Alternatives to Modernism." In *Entering the Realm of Reality: Towards Dhammic Societies*. Bangkok: Suksit Siam, 1997.

Sulak Sivaraksa. *Loyalty Demands Dissent. Autobiography of an Engaged Buddhist*. Berkeley: Parallax Press, 1998.

Sulpicius Severus: *Dialogues*. In Sulpicius Severus et al. *The Western Fathers,* trans. F.R. Hoare. New York: Harper Torchbooks, 1954.

Tidwell, William A., with James O. Hall and David Winfred Gaddy. *Come Retribution: the Confederate Secret Service and the Assassination of Lincoln.* Jackson: University Press of Mississippi, 1988.

Toer. See Pramoedya Ananta Toer.

Trépanier, Esther. *Marian Dale Scott, 1906-1993: Pionnière de l'art moderne.* Québec: Musée du Québec, 2000.

Trilling, Lionel. "Sex and Science: The Kinsey Report." *Partisan Review,* April 1948, 460–76.

Walsingham, Thomas (fl. 1360-1420), ed. Henry Thomas Riley. *Ypodigma Neustriae.* Great Britain: Public Record Office, 1876. Series title: Rerum britannicarum medii aevi scriptores, no. 28, pt. 7.

Weil, Simone, trans. Emma Craufurd. *Gravity and Grace.* London: Routledge and Kegan Paul, 1933.

Weil, Simone, ed. George Panichas. *The Simone Weil Reader.* New York: McKay, 1977.

Weissman, Steve, ed. *Big Brother and the Holding Company: The World Behind Watergate.* Palo Alto, CA: Ramparts Press, 1974.

Wells, H.G. *Mind at the End of Its Tether.* New York: Didier, 1946.

Whitehead, Alfred North. *Science and the Modern World.* Series title: Lowell Lectures, 1925. New York: Macmillan, 1925.

Whitman, Walt. *Complete Poetry and Selected Prose.* New York: Library of America, 1982.

Willey, Basil. *The Eighteenth Century Background.* London, Chatto & Windus, 1940.

Williams, William Carlos, ed. Christopher MacGowan. *Paterson.* New York: New Directions, 1992.

Williamson, Alan. *Introspection and Contemporary Poetry.* Cambridge, MA: Harvard UP, 1984.

Wittgenstein, Ludwig, trans. D.F. Pears and B.F. McGuinness. *Tractatus Logico-Philosophicus.* London: Routledge, 1961.

Wood, Anthony, ed. John Gutch. *The History and Antiquities of the Colleges and Halls in the University of Oxford.* Oxford: Clarendon Press, 1786.

Wordsworth, William, ed. John O. Hayden. *The Poems.* New Haven: Yale UP, 1981.

Wordsworth, William, ed. Jonathan Wordsworth. *The Prelude, 1799, 1805, 1850.* New York: Norton, 1979. Citations from the *Prelude,* unless otherwise noted, are from the 1805 text.

Wright, Kathleen. "Heidegger and the Authorization of Hölderlin's Poetry." In Karsten Harries and Christoph Jamme, eds., *Martin Heidegger: Politics, Art, and Technology.* New York: Holmes & Meier, 1994.

Yates, Frances A. *The Rosicrucian Enlightenment.* Boulder, CO: Shambhala, 1978.

Yeats, William Butler. *Essays and Introductions.* New York: Collier Books, 1968.

Yeats, William Butler. *The Collected Letters,* ed. John Kelly. Volume I, 1865–1895. Oxford: Clarendon Press, 1986.

Yeats, William Butler. *The Collected Poems of W.B. Yeats: A New Edition,* ed. by Richard J. Finneran. New York: Collier Books, 1989.

Zinn, Howard. *A People's History of the United States.* New York: Harper and Row, 1980.

Zinn, Howard. *A People's History of the United States.* New York: Harper and Row, 1996.